MORE PRAISE FOR

UNSUBSCRIBE

"*Unsubscribe* is unvarnished Dharma. With fierce determination and piercing insight, Josh Korda aims to awaken a culture lulled by material comfort and spiritual delusion. Only open this book if you are ready to hear the truth and take on the task of authentic transformation."

—KEVIN GRIFFIN,
author of *One Breath at a Time*

"Inspired. *Unsubscribe* offers a way to radically change your life into wholehearted being. Read. Explore. Engage!"

—SENSEI KOSHIN PALEY ELLISON,
editor of *Awake at the Bedside*

"Josh Korda brings a fresh face to Buddhism. His teachings, grounded in the Theravada tradition, are derived from his personal experience of addiction and recovery. He presents the Dharma in a way that is accessible, engaging, confrontational, and honest. A contemporary sutra for the Dharma-curious and the seasoned practitioner, *Unsubscribe* offers us the opportunity to see the Buddha Way through a new lens."

—SENSEI ROBERT CHODO CAMPBELL,
New York Zen Center for Contemplative Care

"Many of what I consider to be the universal truths are presented in this book, but one thing made *Unsubscribe* really stand out: this book is blunt. And that's exactly what we need it to be. No flowers, no empty promises, just the honest truth."

—MIGUEL CHEN,
author of *I Wanna Be Well*
and bass player for Teenage Bottlerocket

UNSUBSCRIBE

OPT OUT OF DELUSION,
TUNE IN TO TRUTH

Josh Korda

Foreword by Noah Levine

Wisdom

Wisdom Publications
199 Elm Street
Somerville, MA 02144 USA
wisdompubs.org

Library of Congress Cataloging-in-Publication Data
Names: Korda, Josh, author.
Title: Unsubscribe: opt out of delusion, tune in to truth / Josh Korda.
Description: Somerville, MA: Wisdom Publications, 2017. | Includes bibli-
    ographical references. |
Identifiers: LCCN 2017003558 (print) | LCCN 2017033375 (ebook) |
    ISBN 9781614293064 (ebook) | ISBN 1614293066 (ebook) | ISBN
    9781614292821 (pbk.: alk. paper) | ISBN 1614292825 (pbk.: alk. paper)
Subjects: LCSH: Spiritual life—Buddhism. | Buddhism.
Classification: LCC BQ5660 (ebook) | LCC BQ5660 .K65 2017 (print) | DDC
    294.3/444—dc23
LC record available at https://lccn.loc.gov/2017003558

ISBN 978-1-61429-282-1   ebook ISBN 978-1-61429-306-4

21 20 19 18 17
5 4 3 2

Cover design by John Yates. Photograph by Gianna Leo Falcon.
Interior design by Gopa&Ted2. Set in ITC Berkeley Oldstyle 10.5/15.

Printed in the United States of America.

Please visit fscus.org.

CONTENTS

List of Practices   vii

Foreword   ix

Preface   xi

Introduction   1

I. Death Benefits:
Getting Our Priorities Straight

1. Finding Purpose Where There Is None   13

2. How Can We Change?   19

3. Opting Out: Getting over the Fear of Change   27

4. Contemplating Death   37

5. Letting Go of Identity   47

II. Emotional Reasoning:
Understanding Yourself

6. Self-Integration through Mindfulness   59

7. Looking into the Abyss   71

8. Our Personal Emotional History   81

9. Making Room for Difficult Passengers   95

10. No Way Out but Through   113

11. Greeting What Hides in the Shadows   131

12. The Road That We Are Most Afraid to Take
Often Leads to Liberation   139

13. Putting It All on the Line   147

III. Alone Together: Connecting with Others

14. The Importance of True Friends   159

15. Developing Genuine Connection with Others   167

16. Cultivating a Smart Heart   181

17. Cultivating Wise Friendships   193

IV. Opting In for Liberation

18. Seeking the Sublime   217

19. A Mind That Contains Everything   229

Selected Bibliography   235

Index   237

About the Author   247

LIST OF PRACTICES

Facing Our Fears   33

Embracing Change   34

Mindfulness of Death   45

Returning to the Emotional Body   78

Practice: AIM   92

Understanding Compulsive Behaviors   110

A New Relationship with Anger   111

RAIN   126

Noting Emotions in a Safe Container   128

Welcome Mara!   137

Choiceless Awareness   153

Empathetic Connection   164

The Long Exhalation   176

Labeling the Emotion   177

Cleansing Ritual Practice   177

Equanimity   190

Communicating with a Partner   211

Meditation That Leads to the
Transcendent State of Emptiness   224

How Do We Practice When Life Really Sucks?   232

FOREWORD

THE BUDDHA'S TEACHINGS are perfect in all ways and
will lead any who thoroughly applies them to a profound transformation. Josh Korda is a beautiful example of
the transformation that takes place when Buddhist practice (Dharma) is undertaken. The deep personal suffering,
trauma, and confusion that led him to the path and practice
of recovery, Buddhism, and transformational psychology
turned out to be a blessing that he is now sharing with the
world.

In the lineage of Dharma Punx, Josh has integrated the
rebellious and uncompromising ethic of rejecting the status
quo with the disciplined and systematic training of the mind
and heart.

As modern American Buddhists we are in the rare and fortunate position to not only receive the Buddha's Dharma, but
to also receive the dharma of psychology. With his teachings
and this wonderful book, Josh joins the emerging trend of
integrating the best practices of Western theorists with the
highest wisdom of the Buddha.

Josh shows us through his direct experience the process
of healing and awakening. He also has the rare and useful

ability to bring humor and levity to this very serious and important process.

Josh and his wife, Kathy, have helped so many thousands of people with their stewardship and guidance of the New York City Dharma Punx and Against the Stream community. Countless beings have also benefited from his podcasting.

I am proud to call him a friend and a colleague. Together may we continue to make the Buddhadharma available to all who seek it.

Noah Levine, author of *Dharma Punx*,
Against the Stream, and *Refuge Recovery*

Vinny Ferraro, Josh Korda, and Noah Levine:
the three empowered Dharma Punx teachers. Photo by Sarit Rogers.

PREFACE

AS I MAKE SOME final touches to this book in the early
days of November 2016, I cannot help but note the
storm clouds looming in the background of this endeavor.
A recent, ominous cluster of world events: traumatized ref-
ugees flee war-ravaged Syria, seeking any form of humane
reception by Western countries; Asian financial markets
tumble, rattling global markets; a number of far-right-wing
nationalist parties throughout Central and Eastern Europe
rise in popularity; England startles the world with an isola-
tionist, Brexit vote; the United States, never to be dramati-
cally outperformed, always seeking the spotlight of history,
elects a bigoted sexual predator as president.

These words are also forged amid the shadows of essentially mundane, yet still painful personal issues: My sciatica
has flared up again, and so the hours spent leaning over my
laptop, typing out clusters of words, changing them back
and forth with often dispiriting results, causes pain from my
lower back to hip to thigh. My elderly cat Iggy lies nearby,
in the last stages of life, with 10 percent kidney function,
anemia, pressure sores, and infections, requiring intravenous
liquids to stay hydrated and drugs to induce an appetite for

food; he spends his days in what appears to be end-of-life meditation. Trying to maintain a large but essentially anarchistic Buddhist community in New York offers a recurrent array of obstacles and headaches; space usage fees for our meetings continue to spiral, yet our practitioners are often financially struggling, and I, as a Buddhist teacher, live entirely off their contributions. It can be a mess.

In the hours I set aside to assist and comfort individuals from the New York Dharma Punx community with the tools of the Dharma, I am confronted with a multitude of symptoms: PTSD, hypervigilance, dissociation, addiction, chronic depression, self-harm, and so on, invariably stemming from some form of childhood developmental challenges or abuse. These practitioners are no different from me, emotionally activated by the inevitable setbacks of life, as well as the ongoing parade of disturbing news headlines.

But my goal here is not to depress the reader. All of the aforementioned challenges and concerns, mundane or otherwise, embody the core theme of these pages: All of us suffer, and by trying to achieve peace of mind and security by trudging down capitalism's Yellow Brick Road of workaholism, careerism, consumerism, fame seeking, and social-media-reputation fixation, we waste what little time we have, and wind up absolutely nowhere, not even treated to a glittering, extravagant spectacle such as Oz. Trying to acquire or achieve security and serenity keeps the economy buzzing, chews up our resources, and turns us into competitors, mistrusting each other, viewing each other as obstacles, fighting over slices of an ever-dwindling cake.

Still, some might retort, if I play the game well, my efforts may be paid off handsomely; I'll live in a lavish Tribeca condo, complete with a heated rooftop pool with stunning views, lower level parking, fitness centers, a steam room. Yet such a reward offers little, if any, protection from the vagaries of the cosmos. As the Dharma so consistently notes, the world has always been a dangerously unstable place where rampaging calamities spring out of the blue; one's health can fail at any time, fame abruptly shifts its spotlight to others, wealth can be quickly depleted via sudden market downturns, our reputations can be ruined by gossip. It's all so utterly beyond our control. Note how the Buddha's follower Ratthapala, in the sutta bearing his name, summarized the teachings when asked by King Koravya:

> "Sir, there are four statements that can summarize the Dharma:
>
> - Eventually everything in the world is swept away. Nothing endures.
> - The world is not safe; it offers no shelter, nor anyone to provide lasting protection.
> - Nothing in the world is ever truly owned, for when we die, we leave everything behind.
> - The world isn't enough to satisfy a mind lusting for things."

In the *Attadanda Sutta* the Buddha summarizes his experiences in the materialist world as follows:

"I saw people acting like fish flopping about in
    drying up, shallow pools,
Competing for scraps, hostile to one another, and
    became alarmed.
It was a world completely lacking in meaning, prac-
    tically shaking in its vulnerability to change.
So I longed for a place that was safe but saw that
    that didn't exist either.
With so much conflict and competition, I became
    distressed.
And so I sought peace of mind in another manner
    entirely."

The result of trying to consume happiness via Amazon
is the demise of a few other things, such as egalitarianism,
freedom of thought, and social purpose. In the course of a
couple of decades we've moved from connecting with each
other by hanging out on stoops and in parks to posting selfies on Facebook and snarky comments on Twitter. As they
say, the silence we receive for all these efforts is deafening.
One doesn't need to be a psychologist to discern that constant busyness is a symptom of avoidance, for when we run
out of fuel and idle to a full stop, what do we experience? The
voidness of meaning that is simply surviving in this world.

If we're lucky, eventually we may stumble upon a powerful, if devastating insight: *having more only leaves us wanting more.* The samsaric cycle of craving is a thirst that can
never be quenched; the world is not enough to satisfy our
craving. Alienated from consumerism, we may try to locate

alternative ways to achieve some peace of mind. Foraging through the jungle of information provided by the internet, with its multitude of blogs and ability to Wikipedia this or Google that, fosters a belief that information alone might offer the higher meaning we seek. But filling the mind with information is really a variation of seeking security by lining our pockets or filling up our living rooms with gadgets and flat screens, for whether we are accumulating information or consumer goods, *the underlying premise is that the answer is somewhere out there, not available to me already*—this is the belief that fuels craving.

So how do we develop any calm, much less a purposeful, meaningful life, given such a stark proposition? Certainly, the answer is far more complex than sitting on a cushion for twenty minutes each day, breathing. Yes, that will reduce some of our stress, but is that all we can ask? The teachings suggest that what really matters in life, what produces the most lasting impact, are not the situations and circumstances we face—be they dismaying world events or life's challenging obstacles and setbacks—but how we respond to these conditions. If we react by trying to acquire something to save us, we're setting ourselves up for disappointment; instead, we must turn to core assets that are readily available. Then, our lives will change:

(1) **We skillfully prioritize our goals**—the Buddha called this *right understanding* and *right intention*—away from the materialist concerns over our financial security and reputation, toward more existential questions, such as

"What matters in my life given my mortality?" which help us establish a sense of meaning and purpose.

(2) **We understand and integrate our feelings and emotions into our problem-solving routines**, so that we can take into consideration all of our core needs. As neuroscientists and neuropsychologists have amply demonstrated—Antonio Damasio, Joseph LeDoux, Iain McGilchrist, Allan Schore, Jaak Panksepp, and Michael Gazzaniga, to name a few—wise, successful choices cannot be made by producing a stream of language-based ideas; wisdom requires learning how to recognize and coordinate all the nonverbal messages arriving from sources below our consciousness, signaled to us via the emotional body and mind.

(3) **We connect authentically with those around us.** By listening to others without defensiveness and learning how to safely disclose our needs, we forge the deepest bonds possible, and the social circuits of our brains reward us with all the uplifting, positive emotions toward which we could ever aspire. Connecting with others is challenging, for in opening our hearts to others, we risk being deserted and shunned—which is what we fear the most. But there's really no alternative; openness and honesty are the foundations of trust, and so resilience, even if it's born of the desperation of loneliness, is key. We can develop this skill incrementally, taking calculated risks; that's fine, but take the plunge, it's worth it.

These opening words have established an overview of the practices that we'll elaborate on later. Before we continue to investigate and amplify what has just been offered, however, the reader may well wonder: Just who is the individual writing these pages? What life experiences have led him to such conclusions? Why in the world should I care what he has to say on these subjects? These are legitimate questions indeed, and hopefully the introduction that follows will answer them.

Notes on Translations

All of the versions of Buddhist suttas in this book are my own.

I deeply respect and admire so many of the fine translators working, but I find there's a unfortunate tendency among some to render the early Buddhist transcripts in stilted phrases and word choices, which obfuscates ideas that can actually be quite accessible. Additionally, the language feels stiff, rather than familiar and more vernacular. For example:

> Suppose there is no hereafter nor fruit of deeds done well or ill. Yet in this world I keep myself safe and happy, free from hatred and malice . . .

One would be hard-pressed to understand the Buddha's important, though straightforward message:

> Look, even if there is no such thing as rebirth—if our experience ends with our death—and no way

to feel the results of our actions, it's still worthwhile to act harmlessly, as we'll feel better about
ourselves while we're still alive.

And so, over the years, I've developed my own vernacular
style of presenting the Pali Canon, relying on the other translations as rough guides, Pali-to-English dictionaries, and my
decades of study to fashion my own adaptations. I've found
this helps practitioners become quickly comfortable with the
profound wisdom of the canon. The reader would be well
advised to consult the now-standard translations of Thanissaro Bhikkhu, Bhikkhu Nanamoli, or Bhikkhu Bodhi if they
want to deepen their study.

To protect the confidentiality of practitioners I've mentored
and counseled over the years, I haven't referred to individuals
by their names and, whenever possible, I've chosen to focus
on and disclose my own experiences and struggles, rather
than reveal the experiences others have chosen to share
with me.

Acknowledgments

Without the input of the following individuals this book
either would not have been possible or would have emerged
in a significantly diminished form:

Kathy Cherry, my partner in life and in spiritual practice:

virtually all of the ideas in these pages originated in our conversations and Dharma debates.

Natasha Korda, my brilliant sister who models integrity, kindness, and intellectual rigor.

Noah Levine, the author of *Dharma Punx*, *Against the Stream*, and *Refuge Recovery*, who encouraged me to become a Dharma teacher, oversaw my teacher training, and set a pristine example for how to run a Buddhist community.

Vinny Ferraro, for his wisdom, humor, authenticity.

Ajahns Sucitto, Geoff, and Amaro; Tara Brach; and so many other teachers, for the honor of attending their numerous retreats and for fielding my numerous questions.

The numerous Dharma teachers I've cotaught with over the years who exuded wisdom, including Jessica Morey, Lucia Horan, Melissa McKay, Dave Smith, George Haas, Chris Crotty, Kevin Griffin, Jay Michelson, and so many others.

Laura Cunningham, my editor at Wisdom, and all the other individuals there who played roles—both seen and unseen by me—in preparing this book for the world.

Eva Talmadge and Adam Groff, for their willingness to read through early drafts of chapters and offer so many wise suggestions. Mark Bellusci, Quentin, and other friends for early readings as well.

Rod Meade Sperry and Melvin McLeod at *Lion's Roar* magazine; Emma and all the other fine individuals at *Tricycle*.

And, crucially, the thousands of practitioners, either in Dharma Punx NYC gatherings, or via email after listening to podcasts, whose questions and comments inspired these pages.

May any merit associated with endeavor be directed toward the liberation from suffering of all beings.

INTRODUCTION

MY NAME IS JOSH, I'm a New Yorker and a recovering alcoholic and drug addict. I've lived through some shit in this city over the course of my life. I've been through riots, arsons, and blackouts, stood witness to the birth screams of punk and the slow death-by-greed of once-vibrant neighborhoods, run from the batons wielded by thugs operating under the guise of law and order, and mourned legions of beautiful artists, writers, and musicians lost to a disease that the most powerful man on earth couldn't be bothered to speak about. Over the first four decades of my life, I got fucked up, scraped up, stumbled, fell and got up again, grew up, got older, got married, and settled into a respectable career in advertising in the city.

In early September of 2001 I woke up to a beautiful late-summer morning, optimistic that I had enough of my ducks in a row to live a secure and happy life. On the way to work I overheard a strange conversation on the subway. Extraordinary events were being relayed through the car. When the train arrived at Union Square, I exited and climbed the stairs into a commotion at street level. Following the gaze of the crowd, I looked toward downtown to see tremendous plumes of black smoke erupting from the World Trade Center. When one tower collapsed, we gasped, screamed, and were hit with the shivering realization that thousands were being swallowed, crushed, entombed. I didn't know at that time that a fireman I'd come to know over my years in Alcoholics Anonymous was perishing at that very moment. Soon afterward, the remaining tower was swallowed into the earth as well, leaving an unfamiliar hole in the skyline.

I spent the following months walking about in a trance of confusion, which ultimately resulted in a nervous breakdown. I wandered, alternating between medicated numbness and self-hatred. My self-care during this period consisted of weekly visits to a variety of Buddhist centers, daily twelve-step meetings, morning meditations, and a regimen of antidepressants. This routine might have been enough for most people. But it wasn't for me.

I had to face the fact that I, just like everyone else, was falling through time toward my inevitable death with absolutely nothing to cling to. I was living in a world where nothing was guaranteed and everything could go up in smoke any time. And what the fuck was I doing with my life? Working in advertising?! Working in a vain attempt to accumulate enough capital to alleviate financial insecurity, loneliness, and fear of old age seemed surreal. At some point I had convinced myself that I was making a compromise: work in the biz for a few years, make money, and cash out. The truth is the lure of a solid paycheck, dangled before the financially struggling, is powerful. The truth is I sold out.

And what did the twelve-step programs have to offer?

They work for a lot of people, but all I got were patronizing pats on the head offered by smug true believers who, armed with quotes from the AA Big Book, dutifully insisted that my clinical depression was repayment for my atheism and lack of effort. Desperation finally motivated me to seek my own solutions.

I've had a lifelong fascination with and love for the Dharma and Western psychology. Back in the mid-1970s, my dad, a recovering drunk, suddenly became a Zen Buddhist and dragged me to hear strange Japanese and Himalayan men give Dharma talks. In my early teens I started to read through the Buddhist texts accumulating on our bookshelves—Philip Kapleau's *The Three Pillars of Zen*, Shunryu Suzuki's *Zen Mind, Beginner's Mind*, and Alan Watts's *The Way of Zen*. I'd never lost touch with the Dharma, but now I rekindled my studies in the Buddha's teachings and sought out retreats with monks who embodied the kindness and balance I so desperately needed.

The Buddhist scene at the time was dominated by teachers in the so-called "mindfulness movement." So it comes as no surprise that I seemed to encounter them everywhere I turned. Mindfulness teachers are quick to celebrate internal awareness and the engaged Buddhism of social protest and demonstration, but if you seek their guidance in making significant life changes, like radically rethinking career and livelihood, many grow uncomfortable and switch the subject back to acceptance. It seems that taking the big leaps required for any significant personal transformation run counter to much of contemporary Buddhist practice. Rather

than realistically address the soullessness of capitalist priorities, many of the teachers I spoke with were set on encouraging me to remove the aversion to my marketing job!

The big message of Western mindfulness practice often
plays out like this: If I find my work pointless, I should continually recognize my aversion, label it, allow the experience
to arise, and investigate how I physically and mentally react to
each moment of the experience. It's all impermanent, arising
and passing. If I mindfully embrace the external conditions of
my life and learn to put aside my resistance, I'm assured that
my natural interest will be aroused: I'll learn how to open to
the experience of advertising. "Acceptance is the key" should
be my guide, year in and out. But while this might make
my daily grind less arduous, it fails to alleviate the meaninglessness packed into every second I spend in advertising.

After spending some time with contemporary mindfulness
teachers, a dispiriting realization began to take shape: Buddhist practice has grown rapidly in the West, especially in
this country, partially because it's been revamped into a shape
that's quite chummy with capitalism. I have little doubt that
the world of insurance claims adjusters have realized what
a good deal mindfulness is: give people a couple of meditation techniques, and they'll be able to reduce chronic stress
without continual appointments at the clinic—panic attacks
and anxiety disorders can be reduced without expensive psy-
chiatric bills. Large corporations are starting to hire mindfulness teachers to come in and train stressed-out workers
to stay focused on the programming without melting down.
When I read that mindfulness was being taught in large tech

companies so that programmers can spend eleven-hour days coding without losing their minds, the whole "mindfulness movement" began to feel a bit too convenient to the smooth flow of commerce and capitalism. Big business may appreciate how well mindfulness fits in, but that wasn't particularly welcome news to me.

The great message conveyed by the life of the Buddha wasn't confined to his enlightenment and discovery of the Dharma; it was also in his willingness to take the great risk that preceded, and also made possible, both those events: he opted out. He quit the family job, turned his back on the wealth and riches his birth in the upper classes afforded, and embraced the unknown. He turned away from a life of meaningless obligations and responsibilities, and wandered off into the jungle of Sarnath. For six years he practiced with ascetic devotion, barely surviving on nuts and berries.

There's a lesson here: to attain positive emotional well-being, not to mention a sense of purpose in life, it's not enough to maintain a daily meditation practice in the midst of a life that in no way betters the world. To reach his enlightenment at Bodh Gaya, Siddhartha first had to opt out of the easy life and choose the unknown. To be a spiritual rebel, a Dharma punk, a true practitioner, one has to give the middle finger to materialism, self-centered fear, self-serving luxury, financial security. We have to say no.

Challenging the fetishization of mindfulness in American Buddhism is like examining the proverbial gift horse's teeth and gums; mindfulness attracts many people to spiritual practice, sells books, fills up retreats, and is helpful in institutions such as hospitals, schools, and therapeutic settings where meditative and contemplative awareness practices are a viable alternative to "religious" or "spiritual" interventions. And of course mindfulness does work. It has been proven effective in lessening daily stress and reactivity. I teach mindfulness; it's one of the factors of the Noble Eight-fold Path. But mindfulness alone does not answer the great existential question: What's the point of my existence?

To really get at the guts of the big questions, to wrestle with the world we live in and how we live in it, we need to wisely evaluate our external conditions and may actually have to change them for meaningful transformation to occur. Luckily for me, I found others like myself who sensed what Buddhism had to offer in terms of facing up to the hard questions and challenging the status quo, and who were disillusioned with those who dominated the American Buddhist scene. If you've visited more than a few Buddhist centers, you know the shtick well: meditation instructors who present themselves to a class wearing bland, emotionally pasteurized expressions, speaking in "calmer than thou," whispery tones, their talks sanitized by years spent copying other pedagogues of the same ilk. I sought a teacher who spoke honestly and openly about their own obsessive thoughts and fears, their struggles with addictive impulses and the rest.

Noah Levine's talks when he first moved to New York made a huge impression on me. They were filled with frank admissions of past misdeeds, mention of his brief incarceration, and his continuing, daily struggle to balance sensual pleasure with spiritual practice. Here was a Dharma disclosed through true experience, even the embarrassing or unappealing, in order to speak to the reality that people like me live in. Here was a voice I could trust and connect with.

I quit my stable job to reprioritize and search for a higher purpose. I try to follow the path of the insubordinate and uncompromising, to pursue spiritual work, regardless of financial distress; I became a full-time spiritual practitioner and teacher, in a tradition outside the familiar institutions catering to the wealthy. While finding oneself alienated from one's life is hardly pleasant, and moving against the normative current of the world, "leaping into the void," so to speak, can be unnerving, I feel I am in good company. Dissatisfaction was, after all, what initially motivated the Buddha to walk away from a seemingly secure and comfortable life. Talk is cheap and easy, but to truly transform our lives in the end *we actually need to do something.*

Over the years, as I've worked at myself and reflected on life, I've gleaned a few pieces of wisdom that are worthy of sharing with you in the pages that follow. The first is that we will not find any sense of purpose in our lives if we do not live with authenticity. When the priorities around which we've organized our lives are inauthentic, they eventually wear thin and grow disappointing. Disillusionment with superficiality is a basic building block of Dharma practice that pushes us to discover what it is that we really need in order to find contentment in life. How do we develop and pursue a new set of priorities?

The second is that we cannot transform ourselves independently. Secure, reliable relationships are necessary to support and guide us as we take the risks needed for growth and transformation to occur. Wise mentors and trustworthy friends are absolutely essential to any spiritual journey. We are social animals; we need to stay interconnected if we are to regulate and maintain our psychological well-being. How do we find such mentors and friends? And how do we build and maintain relationships with them?

And lastly, it is our responsibility as spiritual practitioners to reconnect with what we've suppressed, quashed, and silenced within ourselves for the sake of making our lives easy and profitable. The work of the spiritual warrior asks that we put aside all that is hollow, phony, sentimental, and slick, and learn to usefully hold and disclose what is difficult, challenging, ungainly. How do we use honesty and truthful revelation to come to accept ourselves? How do we use honest appraisal of ourselves to see others as they really are? How can we make our vulnerability an asset?

In short, I have come to realize that without authentic priorities, secure relationships, and truly honest vulnerability, significant spiritual transformation cannot occur. These three points are the crux of my own practice—which I will tackle and open up for you below.

My name is Josh, and I'm a recovering alcoholic and drug addict, a New York Dharma punk, gratefully living off the donations of others as an urban meditation teacher and Buddhist mentor. I've lived through some shit in my life: I've struggled, fought, and worked, just like everyone has to, to find peace amid the suffering, loss, and disappointment that life brings. What has ended up mattering most was the tedious and challenging work of sitting in quiet rooms, surrounded by friends, trying to fashion some deeper, authentic purpose beyond the ceaseless, chaotic tumult of history. What I've come to know is that the greatest gift we have is the ability to organize our actions and goals around a set of principles that we establish for ourselves, rather than trying to speak lines and act out roles that have been written for us by soulless institutions and the spiritually weak. The choices that we make are what determine in the end whether we are living an authentic life.

So don't just sit there! Opt out. Take the red pill. Check out of the mainstream and start your own revolution. The chapters that follow explore different ways that we can follow the rebel path.

◀ **I.**

Death Benefits: Getting Our Priorities Straight

FINDING PURPOSE
WHERE THERE IS NONE

TO LIVE WITH PURPOSE requires that we take a risk to create meaning for ourselves.

In his memoir of surviving in Nazi concentration camps, *Man's Search for Meaning*, Viktor Frankl concluded that survival rests upon the realization that life, despite its absurdity, holds an authentic purpose that invariably extends beyond ourselves:

> Being human always points . . . to something, or someone, other than oneself—be it a meaning to fulfill or another human being to encounter. The more one forgets himself—by giving himself to a cause to serve or another person to love—the more human he is.

It's worth noting that pleasure and elation are not synonymous with purpose or authentic meaning.

The single-minded pursuit of comfort and ease is an ultimately selfish behavior, best described as a form of drive-reduction behavior: We all have drives, such as thirst, hunger, sex, a search for survival advantage. If these drives are not heeded, they cause stress until they are acted upon. When they are finally acted upon, we feel a sense of satiation and release. For instance, I'm presently thirsty. When eventually I satisfy my thirst with a drink, I'll feel rewarded. I feel similar things when I buy something that I want, or even check my phone for text messages. These materialistic and reward-oriented behaviors trigger an almost disproportionate emotional response. While eating and drinking might seem to simply fulfill survival instinct, they actually give me the same kind of hedonistic satisfaction as buying something fun; I feel strong and secure.

Unfortunately the buzz—neurally similar to a hit of crack, a toot of cocaine, a line of crystal meth (all of which I explored for myself, thank you very much)—doesn't last. Like any other drug, eventually the high wears off and we are invariably left feeling hollow, yearning for more. What goes up must come down, especially our emotions. It is the foundation of the second noble truth of Buddhism that even acquiring that which we desire will ultimately always leave us craving—and consequently, suffering—more.

Since we are social creatures, joining a group can help us maintain our emotional well-being. But to preserve our connection with the group, we might find ourselves conforming to its social norms. In extreme cases we can virtually abandon ourselves just to stay connected. If we deviate from the norms of our group, we'll experience pressure to conform, whether explicitly or implicitly.

Seeking to fit in and belong can cause our estimation of

satisfaction and happiness to devolve into nothing more than the pursuit of status symbols and social recognition. But the happiness such achievements provide are short-lived. Connecting with others is important for survival and a general sense of well-being, but the urge simply to conform and comply is ultimately just another pursuit of short-term advantage and pleasure. It doesn't give our lives any real purpose.

Feeling a sense of purpose is very different from merely feeling pleasure. A sense of purpose, or meaning, arises in me when emails arrive from complete strangers who have listened to my podcasts and are seeking some words of comfort. I don't simply enjoy the emails. Reading them gives me a call to action, a desire to do something for others. While pleasure provides my *self* what it thinks it wants, purpose transcends my narrow sense of self. Purpose, a reason for being, must connect to one's authentic experience.

We transcend meaninglessness only when we think and act beyond merely trying to satisfy our needs. We become authentic, in part, by extracting ourselves from the norm, adopting values that question rather than mimic, and taking on work that reaches beyond ourselves.

The pursuit of meaning and purpose doesn't support the illusion of security. To find purpose we must take a risk. Helping someone with an illness or addiction, starting a relationship, raising children, or pursuing a meaningful career can require risking both our external and internal resources.

Once we've invested efforts into people and areas outside of our narrow self-interest, we may experience some periods of greater anxiety than people who chase after security and approval. Teaching at a Buddhist community, for example, creates meaning for me but requires sacrifice. I live hand to mouth, making a fraction of the money I made in advertising. And while many believe—incorrectly—that advertising is a glamorous profession, few even have a clue what being a Dharma teacher means, much less display any admiration when I tell them it's what I do. Making life authentic and meaningful doesn't always make us feel secure or comfortable.

Trying to live a life of meaning also connects my present experience to considerations of karma: my thoughts and actions have future implications, as the Buddha noted in the *Kalama Sutta*:

> Suppose there is rebirth as a result of skillful or unskillful actions. Then it is possible that after death someone who acts skillfully will arise in a heavenly realm with a peaceful mind.
>
> But suppose there is no rebirth, there are no future lives that result from skillful or unskillful actions. Still, in this lifetime, one will live free from hatred, ill will, feeling secure and at peace.

A purpose involves considering the future implications of our actions, rather than looking good or sounding pleasant to others in the moment. I am better able to sort out what my purpose will be on the basis of honesty and a dispassionate assessment of myself.

Our lives don't come with a user's manual or even a stated

goal. We arrive into consciousness with a will to live, but no real purpose beyond continued existence. None of us are provided a reason for being beyond survival of the species, which is often less than inspiring. So how do we find meaning in a seemingly meaningless universe? We must create meaning for ourselves. To develop a genuine direction in life we must accept the challenge: We were born without a purpose, so we must create one. I am creating my own purpose, right here. I am creating a meaningful life in writing these words, as this organizes my existence toward the project's completion.

We can take the groundless absurdity of life as a challenge by asking, "How can I create a purposeful life?" Here are some questions that can help us choose our purpose by examining some of our natural inclinations:

- If you had a diagnosis of only months to live, what would you change? What obligations and responsibilities would you put aside? How would you behave differently?

- Reflect on the times you experienced the greatest peace. What do these experiences have in common?

- What are the great ideas you respect from the canon of philosophy or literature or culture? How can you live from this perspective?

- What actions did you undertake five years ago that you feel proud of? What can you learn from these actions?

- What would be your final speech to the world? How would you summarize the important things you've learned in life? What have you discovered about life worth expressing to others?

The answers to these questions can help us gain some insight into our meaningful priorities, higher values, and authentic choices. If we want to establish real meaning for ourselves, the meaning has to come from within. As the Buddha taught, we should not base our beliefs and priorities on what is said to be true, what we've heard from others, but what we know to be true based on our own experience. The Buddha taught that, if our beliefs and values are to be authentic, we must verify them for ourselves. Similarly these investigations should be free from the undue influences of social pressure. As such, quiet, secluded contemplation can provide a worthwhile setting for these core investigations.

Once we test and develop reliable values, we live our lives guided by them, rather than simply surviving in the roles we've acquired at work, or in our families, hobbies, etc. We may find that we are guided by compassion, gratitude, forgiveness, and equanimity.

2. HOW CAN WE CHANGE?

BY 2002 I was no longer satisfied or happy with my work. I was so disconnected from my passion for advertising that I couldn't remember ever having any. Moreover I couldn't see how it served any greater good—how it served others. To make matters worse this discontent made it harder and harder to relate to the people around me who took it seriously. Ultimately I had been at the work so long that I was bored and jaded.

The alienation and sense of purposeless made me just want to quit and walk away. I was further driven by the lure of teaching meditation; my love for that was indomitable. At one point that year, I volunteered to start a recovery meeting with meditation at a halfway house for parolees on Avenue D. I'd drop in on a Thursday evening to find no more than two people waiting for the meeting to start. Quite often one or both would be slouched over on methadone as I gave an overview on breath-counting techniques or body awareness. One meeting I taught to three paroled convicts, all of whom spent the entire class facing away from me, staring at a silent television in the background. Even on these occasions I felt far greater fulfillment and purpose than I did winning an award for creative excellence in advertising. This was clearly the direction I needed to go.

However this transition from ad man to meditation teacher was not an easy change to make. Among other things, I had to consider money; since the time of the Buddha, the Dharma is taught only by donation. To charge for teaching the Dharma is to violate its spirit. It's meant to be available to all, regardless of income, without any pressure to contribute. While teaching brought immediate self-esteem and a feeling of contributing to the betterment of the world, it hardly held any promise of paying the rent or putting food on the table. How would I survive, pay bills, and eat?

I was confronted by this hard reality: If we want change we need to move from vision to action. Without action, our vision is just a fantasy. Taking action to change—in my case, or in any case—is daunting.

It takes a lot of patience and support to make major life changes. Patience—because it is a long path and may take time. Support—not only because social support is good for our moral fortitude, but because being connected to others puts us in touch with a power and a motivation beyond ourselves. In the following sections I give some advice on how to cultivate the patience and support needed to make this kind of change.

Find Work That Benefits Others

A meaningful life is one that connects you with others in a way that contributes to their lasting happiness, as well as your own. The keyword there is *lasting*; work that does not really contribute to the well-being of others, even if it makes them happy in the short term, won't contribute to your own happiness either; selling crack and candy won't make you feel good.

> A practitioner should be able to discern unskill-ful livelihood as unskillful livelihood, and skillful livelihood as skillful livelihood. What is unskillful livelihood? Work that schemes, insults, corrupts, deviously influences and focuses on pursuing personal gain for the sake of gain. This is wrong livelihood. In skillful livelihood one is mindful of self and others. (MN 117)

Start Small and Build Up

While I was an attendant at a retreat, Thanissaro Bhikkhu once said to me, "If you make too many changes at the same time, how will you know which one is creating positive results? If you try out too many things at once, you won't know what's working and what isn't." And sure enough, I found that bringing about my own change had to be a step-by-step, one-day-at-a-time process.

I spent thousands of hours over the following years

learning to present the Dharma, figuring that even if I never got the opportunity to teach, at least I'd thoroughly achieve a new skill. Of course I'd already spent many years studying the Dharma and had met with Noah for his insights, but knowing how to give a Dharma talk naturally was quite a different matter. After a while, I realized that I benefited more from transcribing Dharma talks than from reading. Fortunately the average advertising workday has empty, dull stretches. During the off times, I'd find a talk by a Dharma master on the web, listen to a sentence, hit pause, and then rewrite it out verbatim, as best I could. Over the years I must've transcribed hundreds of talks.

Once you have your own one thing to do, it's helpful to dedicate a limited amount of time to that one thing. You can start out by committing just a few minutes a day to an activity and slowly build up. In my case I devoted no more than ten minutes a day to my transcribing practice; I didn't want to set too high a goal, which might set me up to fall short of the mark and quit out of defeat. Doing only small bits at a time lets you accumulate momentum without putting yourself under too much pressure.

Lastly it's helpful to ritualize the activity; doing the activity in the same way, at the same time, same place, etc., will help reinforce it as a habit.

There you have it: One thing, done the same way, a few minutes a day.

Rely on Wise Friends

Surround yourself with trustworthy, empathic people: warm and wise people you can be open and honest with, who don't try to "fix," "solve," or "shame" you. It is important to have people like this: people you can turn to when experiencing difficult emotions so you can express them safely, people with whom you can talk about your difficulties, who can hold your emotions and allow you to process them. The Buddha said that these kinds of people are the "whole of the path." The Buddha taught:

> Choose your friends wisely, for we become like them; someone who wraps rotting fish in grass makes the grass smell foul. Likewise fools leave their mark. But one who wraps powdered incense in the leaf of a tree makes the leaf smell appealing. Likewise the wise leave their mark.

Put Yourself on the Line

It can be helpful to make a formal commitment to change in front of those you care about, the people whose opinions matter to you. It will encourage you to live up to your word.

When I decided to finally give up drinking, in 1995, I realized that making such a dramatic change was likely to fail, as it had in the past. To prevent this I told people close to me—my kalyanamitta—of the commitment and created a sense of accountability. I'd also check in with my friend Craig, who was starting to give talks at the time too, so we'd keep ourselves on track with our progress of becoming Dharma teachers as well. Social support like this can be invaluable when it comes to learning new behaviors. If I failed I would have failed not only myself, but all of those other people, too.

For others that sort of thing might apply too much pressure and attention, but it is very motivating for me. If this sort of accountability seems right, I encourage you to use it.

Be Nice to Yourself

It's important throughout your transformation that you use the carrot, not the stick, to motivate yourself.

While trying to change yourself for the better, you might find that your inner voice, rather than encouraging you along, is criticizing you and shaming you for every misstep: "What's the matter with you? Why aren't you doing better?" This is the stick. Motivating yourself with this kind of internal prodding creates stress. Eventually you come to associate that stress with the goal itself and you begin to procrastinate to avoid the discomfort. That procrastination is sure to hinder your progress.

In order to build enthusiasm, instead use the carrot: Reward yourself with positive experiences and kindness. As a reward for working on a résumé or application, I would allow myself to indulge in some idle internet meandering, or, more skillfully, I'd walk to a favorite spot, take a break with a warm cup of tea, or listen to my favorite music.

Even when you fall short of the mark, though, it's still

always better to handle yourself with care and be kind to yourself. Beating yourself up will not only cause you unnecessary pain but will hinder your progress as well.

Remember That Change Can Be a Lifelong Practice

Don't expect transformation or success to happen quickly. Some of us may find meditation to be easy at first, especially in its simplest forms of observing the breath or repeating phrases, but while such practices can provide some immediate payoffs, such as serenity, the real insights take many years, if not decades, to experience. As we Dharma punx are wont to say: if you want to see how well your practice is going, take an overview every ten years; any sooner is impatience. It's better to prepare yourself for the long haul by thinking of this change as a lifelong practice. If you try to make progress on a short timeline, it's easy to get discouraged when we don't see the results that we want—as quickly as we want to see them. The truth is that your commitment is not about measurable progress and timetables. You're not finishing a project; you are pursuing a calling.

3. OPTING OUT: GETTING OVER THE FEAR OF CHANGE

TAKING AUTHENTIC RISKS and making authentic choices can be terrifying—how can we put this fear of change into perspective?

The Drudgery of Daily Life

Twenty-first-century American workplaces are by and large false refuges. Rather than providing us with actual security, they simply keep our underlying unease quiet.

Our economy is fueled by the insecurity of having no meaningful safety nets. Some countries guarantee their citizens the right to work, healthcare, parental leave, and leisure time, but America gives no such guarantees. People are chained to burdensome debts and spiraling rents, not to mention a perpetual fear of illness and injury that can lead to bankruptcy. Over the last forty years, we have eroded virtually all of the social safety nets that Lyndon Johnson's "Great Society" legislations once promised. Programs that were started to address healthcare, educational inequality, and urban problems have been entirely abandoned. With the cost of living going up and no appropriate increases in income, the erosion of security keeps many people terrified of quitting jobs that are spiritually bankrupt.

Each year, when I peek at the world happiness reports, the United States no longer scores anywhere near the top ten. We don't even score in the top twenty. We score somewhere alongside industrializing nations. The happiest places to live, according to meta-analysis by the *World Happiness Report*, are Denmark, Norway, Finland, Sweden, the Netherlands. What do all of those countries have in common? Social safety nets that allow people to make significant life choices without fear.

The human mind, however, can get used to even the dreariest circumstances. Spending day after day at our jobs, we slowly become comfortable with not only the lash of insecurity, but also the chaos of it all: the grating complaints of dissatisfied customers, the cacophony of a busy office, the honking of traffic, or the stench of a factory farm or sewer. To what end? Just to hold the feelings of insecurity at bay for a little longer. Ultimately we suffer hours in drudgery and disorder in exchange for a false sense of security.

Today's standard work-to-life ratio essentially ingrains fear and stress; by the end of the day or work week, we're agitated to the extent we demand desensitization, via the numbing pseudo-connections of "liking" something on Facebook, the neural deadening of drugs and alcohol, the vacuity of intimacy-free sex. It's no accident that the history of contemporary capitalism is essentially the history of addiction as well. Some of the first imports of capitalism and colonialist enterprise were tobacco, alcohol, sugar, and caffeine; the very stuff that numbs us or excite us while we labor away our lives in meaningless toil.

Buddhism has always critiqued consumerism as a way of life. One of the Dharma's key insights is that craving only leads to more craving. Shopping, sex, drugs, approval, fame—all are short-term pleasure jolts we habituate to quickly; soon we need to accumulate more and more to experience less and less relief.

The Escape from Daily Life

To make up for the difficulty of daily life, some of us seek material rewards, whether it's a new smartphone, car, or just a bigger paycheck or promotion. Others may think they're smarter than that and instead spend their hard-earned resources on travel, theater tickets, and so on, telling themselves that it is their experiences that make life really meaningful. Some of us might even seek out deep, spiritual experiences—a spiritual tour of India, a mushroom trip in Yosemite—and we feel that we are truly changed. But do the new perspectives you gain really last for months? Did the trip lastingly change how you handle loss, rejection, frustration, and criticism? Have you found a way to experience life while maintaining detachment?

When people take off six months or a year, go on world travels, soak in strange locales and customs, can you guess how long it takes for the weariness and dismay to return once they are home? A couple of weeks. I meet and talk with hundreds of spiritual practitioners after they've returned from pilgrimages. At the time they tell me that collecting new experiences is the ticket to liberation. However we're all still the same person when we come back from vacation, after we've found a partner, or after we've done a retreat. The glow only lasts a little while. Even these deliberately deep experiences don't produce real, needed change.

Therefore, whether we trade our hours for better things, better experiences, or even spiritual journeys, one way or another, we always return to our daily lives, to the insecurity and emptiness.

Change in the Face of Fear

When we understand the perpetual futility of our work-and-escape cycle, it doesn't take long for us to realize that we must reach for something more meaningful. Taking authentic risks and making authentic choices can be terrifying. But if we are to move forward, we have to get past that fear.

For my part I am fortunate that I worked at a lucrative profession and that I never had a family to support, so that I could take the steps to pursue a meaningful life for myself. Countless others, though, have to live paycheck-to-paycheck like they are swinging from one trapeze to another, just a slip away from apparent doom. They deal with it by either trying to stay hyper-alert to keep on top of it all, or barely alert so that they can tolerate it. Either one leads to a desire to make everything go away and, again, to the escapes of consumerism or experience-seeking at best and addiction and pathology at worst.

But while many of us quite emphatically desire to shift our livelihood into a field that cultivates self-esteem and a sense of purpose, perhaps by benefiting others, virtually all such gratifying work requires some form of training or other commitment of time, energy, or money. And here's where the yearning for personal growth reaches a daunting obstacle: a swelling of self-doubt or stalling wherein we drag our feet and equivocate, procrastinating at every turn. The nature of this hinderance? Emotional beliefs.

Each of us holds unconscious personal beliefs, based on early life experiences wherein we felt abandoned, rejected, embarrassed; these events leave wounds that remain vividly painful in the dark recesses of the mind. For example, I worked with a very talented artist who continually put off entering her work into local gallery exhibitions, though she very much wanted to grow as an artist. We investigated her stalling by having her visualize what she would experience if she actually went ahead and submitted her work. At first, she expressed positive images of recognition from friends and a renewed vigor in her work ethic; then, however, deeper associations revealed themselves. Entering work for exhibit would leave her vulnerable to criticism and rejection; she would have to face the dreaded fear that she wasn't as talented an artist as she believed. Indeed, she began to recall occasions in grade school where showing her drawings led to ridicule by other students—painful wounds for any child to bear. So the procrastination actually served a purpose, one dictated by an unconscious belief: it spared her from the possibility of being once again disappointed and hurt.

The Buddha noted the power of unconscious beliefs in a teaching called *yoniso manasikara* (best translated as "deep understanding"), in which he taught that even our most self-destructive habits have hidden, underlying *assadas,* or reasons to exist. If we become introverted in social situations, for instance, its because our innermost beliefs equate getting attention with humiliation.

Unconscious emotional beliefs cannot be "told" they're mistaken, for they are forms of implicit knowledge; as someone who was afraid of water or flying can attest, the fear cannot be rationalized away. We should not criticize or shame our symptoms in any manner.

The path to change is based on an essential understanding of the underpinnings of our fears. Change is scary. In my case it required patiently addressing a wide variety of strong, negative beliefs: I would not be empathetic enough to help others, no one would be interested in my help, and so on. Given my childhood experiences with my dismissive and occasionally abusive father, such fears were actually quite coherent and unavoidable. Nothing would change until I connected with my fear and reviewed with it the various periods in which I risked failure and succeeded . . . my career in advertising was, after all, entirely built on gall, as I had no training or even skills to rely upon when I took my first employment as a graphic designer.

Thankfully, once we expose our unconscious beliefs to all the positive life experiences we've overlooked or failed to emotionally imbed, the fear stops appearing to be necessary for our self-preservation, and the procrastination it evokes no longer serves any purpose and will begin to cease. Any change is possible, if we only understand and acknowledge our fears, rather than resist or fight against them.

Practice:
Facing Our Fears

To address our underlying fear of change, it's important to uncover our concealed fears and allay their concerns without any self-judgement, which would only add more emotional wounds into the mix.

Close your eyes and visualize setting your new endeavor in motion, for example by taking a class necessary for your new vocation. As you imagine the scenario, you might note the physical sensations of fear or uneasiness arise, as well as other disturbing mental images, until a full array of uncomfortable feelings appear. Once the unconscious fear is accessed, stay with it for a short period, then take a deep, relaxing breath, release the image, and open your eyes.

The next step is to imagine a different scenario: an experience in life in which you took a risk and felt rewarded or successful. (If, after reflecting over a period of time, no memory appears, you may instead conjure up an entirely imagined event). It's important to linger on positive images for long periods; our neural circuits can imbed negative incidents in less than half a second, but positive occurrences require much longer durations—as much as half a minute for each image—to become moored in our memory circuits.

The deeper purpose we seek does not have to be limited to what we do to bring in a paycheck; it can be found in activities that connect us to others in meaningful, goal-directed interactions. Similarly, silent retreats and secluded meditations are just a part of my spiritual journey. It's only when an activity allows me to connect with others—authentic exchanges of genuine, spontaneous, human feelings and emotions—that the spiritual life lifts me to its greatest heights.

Practice:
Embracing Change

Maintaining an awareness of the ceaseless flux and change of human experience helps us to face the fearsome nature of change by simply familiarizing ourselves with it.

Take a stroll down any street at an unhurried pace, putting aside any sense of destination or time constraints; simply let yourself walk without a goal; don't allow your mind to be overly fixated on memories or plans or idle fantasies, which will lure you away from the surrounding sensations. Allow the sights and sounds of the street to saturate your awareness, trying to stick with the actual experience. Note the passing of traffic, horns, city life, or of birds, dogs, and lawnmowers. Then start to focus on the internal states shifting beneath each encounter: the changing rhythms of inhalation and exhalation; the feelings of comfort and discomfort arising in the stomach, chest, shoulders, throat, and face; the shifting moods of the mind—often distracted, sometimes vigilantly alert, attention modulating from unsettled and jumpy to untroubled and clear.

The closer we observe our internal states, the more profound our awareness of the unreliability of all experience. There is nothing to hold on to for stability; all events that appear, either internally or externally, are in the process of passing. We are falling through space and time, but without a ground to eventually crash against. We are falling, forever.

4. CONTEMPLATING DEATH

Living in the Shadow of Death

DEATH IS INEVITABLE. And may arrive even sooner than we dread. A truth is revealed in the precariousness of the human condition, in the body's vulnerability to infection, disease, and injury: mortality is not the result of fortune or a world gone awry, but a consequence of life itself. While it has been established that we are living in the safest era our species has known, a long life is never guaranteed. While we make assumptions about our safety and life expectancy, and we eat bran and install fire alarms in the hopes of bettering our odds for longevity, our existence is only a blood clot or viral infection away from extinction.

How we relate to this certainty determines how authentic, meaningful, and purposeful our lives are. The more we deny the inevitability of death, the more we will make decisions that are shallow and incomplete. Think of how painful it will be when we're confronted with imminent death—in an accident, or when a disease is diagnosed—and we realize that we have traded far too much for apparent emotional or financial security.

We can't truly understand this truth using rational thought, in part because that same rational thought helped us to justify so many bad choices; rational thought tells us that the job we hate pays the mortgage or the partner we don't love is a good person who's nice to our friends. This truth reveals itself by raw experience: We must experience loss.

For me, experiencing 9/11 woke me to the realization that I was enacting purposeless rituals, fulfilling empty obligations taken on without considering that life can end without the slightest forewarning. As I turned away from the plume of smoke emanating from the remains of the World Trade Center, trying to find my way back home to Brooklyn—most of the bridges were closed, the subways shut down—I felt like I was in a trance, only partially alive. And over the course of the next few months, the full despair set in: my life was devoid of real meaning.

Mindfulness of Death

While contemplating our own mortality can seem to be a downer at best and downright depressing at worst, reflecting on it is a terrific way to investigate our priorities and routines.

When I decide whether or not to take on a project, if I don't weigh the commitment against my time limitations, given the certainty of death, I make the choice without fully considering the real implications. I have only so much time left; is this job, or relationship, or life circumstance, really how I want to spend it? Every significant choice we make should, in one way or another, be evaluated against the Buddha's first noble truth of life: the inevitabilities of old age, sickness, death, and separation from the loved.

Thinking about death also puts resentment and bitterness in perspective. It helps us practice forgiveness and have compassion for the mistakes of others because we realize that time is short. We can relieve ourselves of the resentment and bitterness that we carry through life as so much inner chatter, stress, and hostility. In letting go of resentment, we also acknowledge that we have made mistakes for which we must forgive ourselves, if we are to live free of shame and remorse.

Reflecting on the inevitability of death and the fragility of life doesn't mean that we will choose a lifestyle of hedonistic, immediate gratification. More likely, we will consider the real value of our time spent. We might take the time to find more invigorating employment or cut down our work hours, or it might simply change the way we relate to our responsibilities exactly as they are. We may become more attentive to our loved ones or spend more evenings with friends. The understanding of death opens up new possibilities for life, rather than keeping me plodding along the same path, day in and out, hemmed in by ingrained routines and misguided beliefs.

Death provides the most truthful perspective on how to live. When it comes time to die, we'll care more about what we've done for others and what contributions we've made than we will about how much money we have. We want to look back and see an authentic and meaningful life.

The certainty and unpredictability of death sheds light on life's meaning and priorities. So why wouldn't you spend a

DEATH BENEFITS: GETTING OUR PRIORITIES STRAIGHT

lot of time thinking about it? Because our denial of death allows us to remain deluded, preoccupied, and distracted by unfulfilling bullshit. Living any day as if we've been guaranteed countless more lies at the heart of our delusion and out-of-whack priorities. The natural tendency to ignore our mortality is a tool we use to get through another day without meaning. Our refusal to acknowledge our imminent death is also an obstacle to staying present and connecting to our reality at this moment. For this reason, spending a whole life living in the denial of death would be both tragic and dishonorable.

Living with Awareness of Death

An awareness of death shouldn't be crippling. It is, after all, an acceptance of the inevitable, the reality we harbor within. It requires that we evaluate and reevaluate our priorities, but it doesn't mean that we should live in fear.

Some see death as looming darkness. But we can also see it as a darkness that lights our path in a different way—it can lend gravity and import to otherwise weightless, meaningless moments, and it can free us from caring about needless chores and meaningless frustrations.

While I certainly do not look forward to its arrival, the recollection of death need not be a matter of dread. Yes, it's a reminder that no matter what path I follow, the destination is the same: that time when I can no longer act, think, or feel. And yes, the awareness of death can create feelings of vulnerability and dread. But while I may not like to dwell on my fragility, in every moment I enact it nonetheless. And to pretend life is not fragile and without guarantee is just another way of admitting it, for in the denial of mortality I acknowledge how difficult and challenging it is for my limited psychic faculties to process.

However, *immortality would not solve the problem of life*; unending life would deprive us of the absolute against which all our decisions and choices are weighed. What meaning would sacrifice, love, or creative efforts achieve if they were simply another set of actions spewing out of existence without end? Moments and deeds would be drained of all weight or meaning. Life without death is life without meaning or purpose. Were my time on earth to continue perpetually, life would simply be weighed against exhaustion, which is hardly a superior arrangement.

So the question that confronts me is this: how do I live within the framework of a meaningless world and a looming death? How do I incorporate what is unavoidable yet uncertain as to its time of arrival?

I am tasked with fully opening into each moment, yet I cannot allow myself to be swallowed by the moment; I must write these words against the fullness of the project itself, which implies a future. To live entirely in this moment would mean I would have to relinquish caring about the results of this action as it plays out. I must act as though this moment might be my last, but I also must take into consideration the moments and actions that might follow. So while I live now, my awareness always slips toward an outcome; again, I am ultimately given meaning by my death.

Death Asks Us to Live Authentically

Staying aware of death helps us to be honest about who we are. Thinking about our mortality forces us to think about the choices we make in life, but it also makes us reflect on our authenticity when dealing with others. The Dharma reminds us that the future is unknowable and speculating about it leads to madness. Our sole connection to that future lies in the quality of our intentions, and there is no greater intention than to live openly, fully, with empathy and appreciation of all that is available.

Keeping death in mind helps us extract ourselves from identifying with the roles we've assumed. Although we are born into an established social structure, we don't need to allow ourselves to be drawn into views that are inauthentic.

I worked with one individual, whom I'll refer to as Debra, who grew up in a family in which her needs for attention and support were put on the back burner, as her younger brother suffered from a long-term illness that drained the energy of both parents. Even before the onset of her teen years, Debra was relegated to a caretaking role, and there was no one available to help coregulate the anxieties associated with high school, socialization, sexual impulses, and so forth. This set the template of Debra's life; in each relationship and friendship she instinctively repressed her own emotional impulses for intimacy and support and invariably prioritized others, managing their feelings at the expense of her own.

Debra's own mortality was never emotionally recognized

and accepted, for she was too busy regulating other people's anxieties as a way to safely maintain each relationship. What broke this pattern was initiating a practice of reflection on death. She meditated with the phrase "one day this body will breath no longer" while observing the sensations of the breath and visualizing how her own aging might play out, so she could acknowledge and express authentic fears and inter-personal needs. Astonishingly, within a few weeks of starting the practice, Debra was capable of standing up for herself in her interactions with a verbally abusive boss. Placed against the recognition of how little guarantee of life she (and we) have, it was no longer worth it to bite her tongue and accept unjust criticism. In her own partnership she became less easy to manipulate as well; when the truth of our own demise is acknowledged, many finally discover the courage to pursue "bucket lists" and refuse to mince words.

Interestingly, I've yet to meet an individual who has lost a job or relationship simply from expressing himself authenti-cally. While many of us believe that stating our needs clearly will invariably lead to rejection, abandonment, or losing work, almost invariably these beliefs are unnecessary, mal-adaptive coping strategies that helped us survive our family systems but keep us disempowered in adult life. Reminding ourselves we don't have the time to waste is certainly one approach to shedding these self-sabotaging habits.

Though the materialistic beliefs our world is founded upon try to push death out of mind, we can open up to life by keeping death in our awareness. It can bring a new sense of our priorities into every choice we make. We might remain in our career, or choose to leave it. We *create* our purpose. We might pursue a more conventional life that follows a well-trodden path, or we might walk away from it all, like the Buddha. Regardless of our specific choices, we are liberated when we open ourselves to the simultaneous certainty and unpredictability of death. Aware of our mortality, we can recreate ourselves in each moment by pondering and pursuing whatever we know to be worthy of our effort, given the very short time that we have.

As there are few transcendent givens, certainties, or absolutes beyond death, we aspire to have a life comprised of choices that are made by weighing our lack of guarantees. In a world without ultimate meaning, filled with "fish fighting for food in dwindling puddles," as the Buddha put it, we create meaning by extracting ourselves from the tendency to identify with the roles we've assumed in the world, the performances we put on to pay the rent and purchase food and clothing.

When we reflect on death, we reflexively consider how we would like to be remembered. It becomes more apparent in this reflection that the more our activities interfere with caring for others, the more we abandon ourselves. If we think now that the way we will be remembered is at odds with our present activities, then we know that something is amiss. For my part I would like to be remembered as someone who was caring, insightful, and creative. The degree to which my life as a Dharma teacher and friend adheres to these principles is the degree to which my life is authentic and meaningful.

Knowing that death is imminent and that I have little time to leave an impression, the lesson is clear.

Practice:
Mindfulness of Death

What does a meditation on death in spiritual practice look like? We might sit quietly for a while, keeping our breath in mind until our attention settles on the physical sensations of inhalation and exhalation in the abdomen or chest, or the sensations of air entering and exiting the tip of the nostrils or mouth. When we're focused, we might slowly, silently repeat a simple thought: "One day this body will stop breathing" or "This breath could be my last."

As we add these reflections, note how the words affect how we attend to the sensations of the breath. We observe how these simple truths, when kept in mind, influence how we perceive our experience. Then we shift our attention to our external senses of sight and hearing: "One day the world will blur as my eyesight fails; the sounds will fade with the loss of my hearing; memories will vanish into remote areas of the mind; all the skills I take for granted will evaporate."

Finally, we might bring to mind the five daily recollections of the Dharma: "I am of the nature to grow old, to become sick, and to die; I will be separated from all that is dear to me; all I really own are the actions I take."

After repeating the five recollections, we might purposely bring to mind our life's dramas—the lingering resentments toward family members, friends, or foes; looming financial bills; or mounting responsibilities—and ask ourselves, when framed by the inevitable, how much do these really matter? Knowing that I will be separated from all I cherish and hold dear, are these little dramas really so critical?

We may find that these recollections change the way we greet the frustrations, setbacks, and travails of life; they may well fade in significance when one's final moments are visualized. Perhaps we will be proud, from this perspective, of the choices we've made, or perhaps some decisions won't fare well under such scrutiny. As all of life moves deathward, we can at least transform our greatest sadness—that we know we must die—into our greatest source of wisdom.

5. LETTING GO OF IDENTITY

WE ALL WANT our lives to mean something, so we build up and cling to an identity, hoping that it will provide meaning. It may just be, however, that we find meaning not in identity, but in letting go of identity.

Over thousands of years we have evolved to be mentally oriented toward symbols and language. As a matter of survival, we have had to transmit information to one another and to future generations. One generation taught the next about hunting, agriculture, making tools, food preparation, etc. Language makes our communication precise and immediate. Were we still primates, we would have to establish bonds and convey relational information by means of grunting and grooming behaviors. Language permits us to exchange elaborate details about our every facet of life.

However, there are some downsides to our use of language. For instance, we have a running monologue in our heads that shapes our understanding of who we are, what the world is, and why it is so. Because our language helps to create important meaning for us, we begin to seek meaning in everything that occurs to us—as a result, we live our lives with an expectation of meaning.

Narrative, language-based ideas allow us to plan for the future and visualize solutions to threats and challenges; they run on the fuel of acetylcholine and dopamine and provide sensations of power, which make us feel safe and alleviate our anxieties of vulnerability and abandonment. Our beliefs and ideas present themselves as protection and salvation, but really inner chatter and language leaves us fully addicted to thinking rather than experiencing, to "figuring out" every challenge, as if life is simply a problem to be solved. Eventually we create a world that mirrors abstract, linear thought: a world of billboards and commercials that reifies wealth and the accumulation of goods and power. In trying to figure out what every experience means, instead of truly feeling, we may just feel a little safer. But thought is only an interpreter that distracts us from the deeper truth: we're not sure why we act the way we do, as so many of our impulses are preconscious and beyond our control.

We feel as though our lives are not simply chance occurrences, that they must stand for something greater. It's not simply that we *want* them to matter; we *need* them to matter. By the simple virtue of our inner monologues, we expect our moments on earth to mean something beyond our sensory experience of them, or the mere fact that they happened. We demand significance. So each of us, as we live our lives in language, want our lives to have a big idea, a depth, a value; we want to matter in some profound way that we can divine with our rational minds, like interpreting poetry.

All of this must surely mean something, right?

Finding Meaning and Purpose

The search for meaning and purpose often leads people to religion. The theistic religions provide believers with an omnipresent power, a presence said to be everywhere. Deities provide excellent security; when we need them, when we are most vulnerable, gods are available to us. They provide refuge in times of danger and support during times of loss. Divine forces provide a secure base from which we can move through the world with less anxiety.

The Buddha didn't deny in that kind of god, though. There are many suttas in which the Buddha schools various gods, such as Baka, who believes his status as a deity is permanent, never subject to end. The Buddha warns Baka that even gods are subject to impermanence. Any survey of the suttas will reveal that the worship of gods is not the answer; liberating ourselves from suffering is our own work. We create the suffering; we must alleviate it.

If belief in an omnipresent deity isn't the answer, we might look for a god within—some part of us that transcends material reality. This is thought to be an essential self beneath—or perhaps behind—all our thoughts, emotions, and feelings. The concept of a core essence within us is very alluring when we are need of security. The Hindus of the Buddha's time believed in a transcendent self they called the *atman*, which was immortal and changeless. For a Hindu the meaning of life was to gain awareness of the atman in order to be liberated.

The Dharma, however, maintains that no such essence can

be located in our experience, and it would be a waste of time to try. Too much of our internal experience—thoughts, feelings, moods, physical sensations—are constantly in flux, appearing and reappearing in different arrangements. Pondering the existence or nonexistence of a lasting identity only results in what the Buddha referred to as a "tangle of thoughts."

It should be noted that Dharma doesn't claim we don't have a self, or what could be called *self-hood*: a subjective, individual perspective of the world that is not shared with others. Self-identity is another matter entirely, though; that proposes constancy, an unchanging essence, such as a set of thoughts or feelings that would be present throughout life, providing an underlying unity. When I can bear to listen to a decade-old recording of myself, prattling on in Dharma talks, I have a *self-hood* while listening, and I recognize the *self-hood* of the speaker, but I really don't *self-identify* with the younger version of me; the perspectives, ideas, feelings, and emotions evidenced in the recordings are substantially different from what I experience today.

In the *Gaddula Sutta*, Buddha says,

> Like a dog that is tied to a stake by a leash keeps running around the stake; in the same way the spiritually naive will believe that a transcendent, lasting self can be found amid the body, feelings, perceptions, mental content [thoughts] or consciousness.

In the *Anatta-lakkhana Sutta*, the Buddha demonstrates that if we pay close attention to our experiences of self—our thoughts, bodies, feelings, perceptions of the world, and sense consciousnesses—we'll find these aggregates are in ceaseless flux. Our bodies are always changing: sometimes energetic, sometimes tired, sometimes ill, other times well. Our feelings switch from the comfortable to the tense or agitated countless times each day. Our sensory experience changes with every second. Our thoughts and perceptions change perpetually. Within all of these, how could anyone find a consistent identity? The truth is that there is no single thread of identity that stretches from birth to death.

The Illusion of Continuous Identity

The illusion of continuous identity is most likely a byproduct of the mind's inner narrator: that is, the internal language-based thoughts that interpret and comment on our ongoing experiences. Neuroscientist Michael Gazzaniga refers to this explanatory faculty as the Interpreter. The role of the Interpreter is to produce explanations, to edit and arrange the incessant parade of internal and external stimuli into a coherent story, complete with views, opinions, meanings. The mind's inner chatter is similar to the voice-over in a documentary film, for it helps us make sense of the flood of experiences in each day of life.

The Interpreter is quite herculean, meeting the monumental, unending demand to translate life's random encounters and unconsciously produced urges and impulses into a lucid tale. Whether it's interpreting dramatic events in the outside world, or our internal flow of perceptions, feelings, moods and behavioral impulses, the Interpreter tries to find meaning, or at least tell a story, even if no discernible pattern exists.

What Gazzaniga's research clearly demonstrated was that the Interpreter often creates entirely incorrect theories and explanations, no matter how dubious. For example, a patient who has had the two hemispheres of their brain separated can be instructed to stand by a window and wave; since this action uses the right hemisphere only, the patient's left hemisphere will have no idea why they waved. If the patient is asked to explain the behavior, the Interpreter, which is a function of the left side of the brain, will with impressive swiftness fabricate a plausible though entirely bogus story: "I saw a friend outside." What's truly fascinating is that the patient has no idea they're essentially lying; the left hemisphere's job is to rationally annotate everything and believe its own stories, even if they're made out of whole cloth.

It is hard to overemphasize how much influence our thoughts have in our perception of experience. Studies show that if we have recently heard or seen the word *eat*, we will likely to fill in the word puzzle "S O _ P" as *soup;* conversely, if we were recently exposed to the word *hygiene*, we'll solve the same world puzzle with *soap*. Should I encounter a California condor, if my first thought is "a vulture-like predator with a nine-foot-long wingspan," my reaction to the bird, including my memory of it later, will be far different from if

I added the thought "a majestic, endangered species with a population of only 230 living in the wild."

Likewise, if I annotate the disappointing news that my elderly cat has a terminal kidney illness with "Why are so many bad things happening to me right now?" I will feel alone in my disappointment and won't reach out to others to share my sadness. I might even be less caring for the animal than if I interpret the news with "This sucks, but it was bound to happen eventually."

The Interpreter, due to our indoctrination into the dominant Western cultural ideas throughout our family interactions, our education, our bombardment with mass-produced culture, primes us toward a number of particular beliefs and actions:

- Self-sufficiency must be maintained at all costs ("I know how to take care of myself, thank you very much!"), whereas dependence on others is derided.

- Accumulation of social recognition, perhaps even fame, is worthwhile, whereas the obscurity of quietly working toward the benefit of others is humdrum.

- Being the "life of the party" means we've had a good evening, whereas spending the time listening to others means we "sat in the background."

- Perhaps the greatest delusion of all: I am a wholly unique individual with a core personality that stays consistent throughout life; in other words, I have a lasting identity. The Interpreter's explanations create the sense of an abiding and consistent self—an identity that's controlling all of our actions, authoring all of our decisions—the illusion of continuity where there is actually a fluid, shifting, changing stream of neural events.

The search for a lasting identity is a stressful waste of time; it's disappointing to keep looking for something that doesn't exist. The more we seek our true nature, our underlying identity, the more we find it slipping away. Sooner or later we experience a thought or feeling that doesn't fit into the scheme we've constructed. The mind is like a river through which everything flows eventually; we can have hideous, wicked thoughts one moment and in the blink of an eye have thoughts as compassionate as the Buddha's. Searching for a transcendent self amid our personal experience is a Sisyphean endeavor at the very least.

However, this doesn't mean that we have no kind of self at all. We each have a conventional identity that allows us to function in the world. We go to work and perform the tasks that keep us employed. I have a name and so do you. When I introduce myself to someone, I don't launch into a diatribe about not having a transcendent identity; I introduce my conventional self.

But the self I feel right now as I type is not going to be the same self I experience when I sit down to meditate, or check my emails, or settle in to watch a movie. I will experience each of these settings from a different perspective, or shade of personality. If I ever believed in an enduring self, it's now barely possible; I can barely listen to my Dharma talks from the last decade, as the thinking process I hear is now utterly foreign to me.

The Buddha said there's something liberating and joyous derived from letting go of the fierce belief in self.

We change how we think and act depending on the settings in which we find ourselves. When we stop attending to our inner monologue and really pay attention to what we're saying and doing, we make an interesting discovery: we behave differently when we feel safe and secure from when we're uncomfortable. When we are around strangers, for instance, our self-consciousness makes us somewhat controlled and guarded. When we feel secure, loved, and accepted, we are uninhibited by self-consciousness and more open to things. The less self-conscious we are, the more we engage the world around us. We can dance or play, be creative, funny, or serious; emotional, passive, or intellectual. When we are secure, more fluidity and playfulness emerge.

The search for self is a yearning to be anchored, tied to meaning, while the world, both external and internal, shifts and changes. By trying to create something enduring in the midst of change—a permanent self—something which itself always ends up changing, we end where we started. But if we give up the search for permanence, we can release the feelings of insecurity.

The point may lie instead in seeking meaning relationally, in the secure attachments with others that allow us to open spontaneously, to connect and create from an unguarded place. The meaning we've been looking for may reside in the last place we expected to stumble across it—not in identity, but in letting go of the demand for identity.

◀ **II.**

Emotional Reasoning:
Understanding Yourself

6. SELF-INTEGRATION THROUGH MINDFULNESS

Mindfulness of the Body and Emotions Leads to Self-Integration and Away from Self-Sabotage

IN LIFE we rely heavily on what could be called the "representational'" capabilities of the mind to assist us in making all our important decisions. Let's investigate how this works.

Occasionally I receive emails describing interesting teaching opportunities: "Josh, we would love you to come teach at our new Dharma center!" The message describes the center, its size, community, location, which time slots are available, how much of my travel expenses they could cover, and any number of other details. When it's time for me to decide whether or not to pursue the opportunity, I might feel inclined to "figure out what to do": switch on the neural circuitry that allows me to visualize a sequence of images involving traveling and teaching at a place I actually haven't seen or visited. In essence I'm projecting what a future experience might entail, based on assumptions, cobbled-together images from previous experiences, imagination, expectations, and so on.

Another example: When I'm burdened by financial or interpersonal obligations, undetermined schedules, missed appointments, and so forth, my first inclination is to create an array of speculative visual images and thoughts, little movies that portray "ways out" of my present dilemmas. One movie shows me hopping on a plane to southeast Asia—moving to a remote tropical beach where I envision life's dramas left behind, all tension resolved. I shrug off such quick fixes: they're too escapist, and unlikely, given all the ties that bind me to Brooklyn and my spiritual community. Next I may imagine telling off those individuals I believe are getting in my way. Once again I decline this solution, perhaps from an unhealthy tendency to avoid conflicts, or perhaps from a wiser realization that these individuals aren't responsible for the tension I'm feeling, that my discomfort with unresolved issues lies at the heart of my present suffering.

What I'm doing in these examples is representing the world in my head. I'm painting an internal version of the world, so that I can play out possibilities and work through different possible scenarios, all to reach a decision.

It's easy to be unaware of how much we rely on abstract representations of the external universe to make choices and decisions. And representations help us with more than just choices; abstract thought allows us to replay life's confusing or overwhelming events over and over, so that we can find some form of coherence or meaning that wasn't originally apparent. After breakups, conflicts, stressful encounters, and disappointing news we replay the experience, trying to figure out what it all meant, what went wrong, how we can avoid bad news in the future.

What we generally fail to realize is that representational

thought is often largely the product of the left hemisphere of our brains, which prioritizes accomplishment, accumulation, and manipulating the world to our advantage, at the expense of the right hemisphere's needs, which emphasize maintaining secure interpersonal attachments and personal safety.

The analytical, planning, and organizing circuits also have another tendency that should be noted as well: In re-presenting the world, our thoughts tend to reduce new experiences into familiar concepts and beliefs: what the Buddha called *sanna,* or preexisting perceptions of the world. In the Pali Canon, *sanna-vipallasa,* which roughly translates as "distortions of perception," refers to the degree to which the world is misperceived and altered as we transform actual, sensory-rich experience into disembodied ideas for our thoughts to manipulate. For example, if I view any possibility to teach as beneficial to building a reputation as a Dharma teacher, then the *sanna* associated with teaching will lead to positive visualizations of any opportunity. I'll overlook whether or not the occasion is, for example, ethically sound (I've received countless offers to teach at large corporations, which I invariably decline). Every time I rely on representational thought, I'm flattening the world into simplistic personal associations, which primarily consist of old distorted ideas. So much for "thinking our way out" of situations.

The more we try to problem solve by relying on narrative thought, the more we're likely to prioritize financial gain, awards and titles, and achievements over our needs for love, community membership, and empathetic connection with loved ones.

A study by Matthew Killingsworth and Daniel Gilbert called "A Wandering Mind is an Unhappy Mind" noted that we spend almost half of our lives thinking about things other than what we're doing; instead we're creating alternative realities in our minds to help us worry, fantasize, and remember. The study additionally demonstrated that such speculative/representative cognition generally tends to leave us stressed and unhappy. Perhaps this is because when we're not present, we quickly lose awareness of our feelings and emotions; many of our trains of thought take us nowhere good.

But neither you nor I have to rely on the representational circuits as a primary tool for making decisions and navigating through life; the best way to "process what it means" isn't necessarily to imagine the past or the future. The circuits that translate our rich, embodied experience into words and ideas are only a small part of our cognitive capabilities. We love the idea that our thought is at the epicenter of the mind, controlling our behaviors and impulses, but, as the Buddha noted in his causal chain of suffering, thought arrives after feelings and impulses, both of which we're generally quite unaware.

Furthermore, a lot of the suffering in our lives comes from trying to think our way through everything while disregarding the important information our emotions present. While we may be tempted to believe that logic, planning, and organization, in conjunction with meditation and spiritual reflection, should be enough to navigate through life, our emotions aren't useless. They are important messages, sent via physical impulses, felt urges, body states, and nonverbal cues from the unconscious mind—which prioritizes security and connection over ambition and achievement.

If I could summarize my work as a Buddhist teacher and mentor into a single unifying goal or theme, it would be providing people with the many tools of the Dharma that allow us to *translate and integrate the emotional mind into our conscious, ambitious life agendas.* In every situation in life we are of at least two minds: one that consciously interprets events through language and ambitious narratives, reviewing how each event will fit into our plans for the future, and one that is unconscious, deciphering experience in terms of our connection to the pack. In order to pay proper attention to the latter, we must develop awareness of all the nonverbal elements of our internal experience—such as our breath, gut feelings, and moods—so that we may consider the needs they're expressing: never-ending hopes for love, connection, emotional support.

When it comes time to decide whether or not to accept a teaching opportunity, in order to integrate both halves of my mind, I may turn my attention away from narrative, representational thought, focusing my attention instead on the actual experience of stress itself: the uncomfortable breathing comprised of fast inhalations and shallow, incomplete exhalations; the sensations of muscles in the stomach and shoulders contracting; my jaw locking tight and my forehead muscles pulling taut; my attention jumping about from one idea to another. And so I let go of addressing life as if it's a set of problems to be solved, and address what's actually present. I've moved from a "top-down" cognitive approach

EMOTIONAL REASONING: UNDERSTANDING YOURSELF

to resolving life's suspense or uncertainties (thinking my way out of challenges) to a "bottom-up" process (becoming aware of the physical and mental states that constitute the actual experience of worry, boredom, discomfort, and so on). I will likewise investigate what lies beneath neutral and positive experiences as well.

This is a systemic approach to refocusing the mind away from external concerns (which can feel insurmountable) toward an internal awareness of the agitation itself. After all, it's far easier to control one's breath and relax one's muscles than it is to control other people, no?

It's important to remember, however, that such mindfulness is not a form of acquiescence or resignation. It doesn't mean we agree with the conditions around us, that we won't quit jobs we hate, that we concede that radical change cannot happen in our lives. Indeed, I've found that deeply investigating an experience, even the profoundly mundane and meaningless, is to pay attention to how I really feel while I'm there, in the salt mines, wasting away my precious minutes and hours—and this shows me what I need to do, to change, to get out.

The Four Foundations of Mindfulness and the Parts of Your Brain

If we are to practice such a fundamental cognitive shift, from external vigilance to internal awareness, it helps if we investigate the different systems of the mind in a succession of stages. Many of the processes of our minds are generally spurned as uninteresting, left outside the spotlight of conscious attention, even though they have profound influence over our choices, behaviors, and the very shapes of our lives.

So let's start with what keeps us breathing, thermally regulated, and digesting food, all while we attend to headier, more elevated concerns: the brainstem and hindbrain, which are the oldest parts of the brain. They organize our core movements; thanks to these regions we can breathe without oversight.

The breath is a very important tool for keeping a steady stream of oxygen in the body, but it's also a way to develop peace and to maintain calm. In fact, many of the aims that bring many of us to spiritual practice can be addressed by bringing our attention to how we are breathing.

Our brains are set to a needlessly high default level of threat detection, even though we as a species have never been safer, due to advances in medicine and efficient storage of food supplies, and perhaps the systemic eradication of our predators. Evolution, however, has not kept up the pace, and so we're wired for survival the same way we were tens of thousands of years ago, when the world was a significantly more dangerous place to survive. So our stress levels are way too high, considering that most of us will probably not be chased and consumed by predators. Chronic stress can lead to a variety of health problems: impaired immune function, digestive issues, diabetes, etc.

When we bring our attention to the breath and gradually lengthen the exhalations, we essentially lower our threat sensitivity level to a far less vigilant state, which leads to long-term health benefits. We lower our heart rates, relax, and make eye contact and attune with others; we increase our ability to focus and maintain calmness and decrease anxiety.

Thus, even though we may not consciously notice them, the oldest systems of the brain profoundly influence our current experience. And appropriately enough, the first foundation of mindfulness is awareness of the body, for which the breath is a good entryway.

Once we have become familiar with the quality of our breath, the Buddha has us shift awareness to the body; as described in the *Four Foundations of Mindfulness Sutta*, we become aware of the sensations associated with our present state, whether we are "walking about, standing and looking around, bending down or extending our limbs in any manner, while eating, drinking, chewing and tasting, during urination and defecation, talking, and remaining silent . . ." Bodily experience provides a primary channel for self-care. In paying attention to the sensations of body—Are my shoulders relaxed or tightened? Are my palms relaxed or gripping? Am I looking straight ahead or is my head habitually tilted downward?—it becomes possible to address functions of the brain that maintain psychological disorders. Therapies that focus on a patient's physical sensations, for instance, have proven very effective at treating PTSD. Once again, we are working from the bottom up rather than top-down.

The second foundation of mindfulness is mindfulness of feelings and sensations.

Strong physical sensations known as *gut feelings* or *somatic markers* are often signals from the right hemisphere of our brains, which is exceedingly connected to the body and tends to express itself physically more than the left hemisphere does. The right hemisphere is the seat of our emotions and governs how we behave in our interpersonal affairs; the left is the realm of abstract, representational thought. The activity of the right is often perceptible to us if we note our bodily sensations. For instance, we can pick up on the presence of an underlying emotional state by noting the muscle groups in the front of the body; there is a cluster of nerves that connects the brain stem to the muscles of the face, throat, heart, and abdominal region, which is why we can physically experience separation from others as "heartbreaking," and fear as "gut wrenching."

If we note the feeling-states of our body in times of stress or while making a decision, it will help us to become aware of, and take into consideration, our fears, desires, and needs.

The third foundation of mindfulness brings our awareness to the moods of the mind: noting how we focus our attention, keeping tabs on emotions that are arising and passing. As the Buddha explained, "Know when the mind is infused with lust and when it is without lust; know when the mind is infused with hate and when it is without hate; know when the mind is unaware and when it is aware; when the mind is confined or spacious, distracted or present, transcendent or caught up, calm or agitated . . ."

The right hemisphere is far stronger when activated than the left, and noting where we're focusing our attention is often a clue to our emotional state. For instance, while going through a break up, we may go to a party and spot our ex. We may not want to think about them or even pay attention to them—we might tell ourselves we're not interested in what they're doing—and yet we'll find their movements and activities commandeering our attention. Our left brain is battling with our right.

The way I look at others, whether I'm sustaining eye contact or looking down, the tone of my voice, the gestures I make with my hands, my body posture—all of these signal my emotional state of being: Do I feel vulnerable and in need of care; do I feel angry and need space? Outside of the words we speak, we're communicating all the time, but these messages are largely being activated unconsciously. They're generally not under conscious control but we can bring awareness to these behavioral signals, and thus increase our own self-awareness and communicate more skillfully with others.

Finally, we arrive at the circuits that sustain long-term goals, stories, and abstract logical concepts. This is where we find Michael Gazzaniga's Interpreter, which we discussed in chapter 5: the inner chatterer in one's mind; the ideas that explain the world to us, that make sense of our actions. This ongoing stream of internal commentary, views, opinions, and rationalizations create the illusion that our thoughts are creating, producing, authoring, and controlling all of your actions. As the Buddha noted, and which has been subsequently documented by neurologists, thought is very, very late in the timeline of neural events; well before we think about how to speak or act, the faster circuits in the brain—which we've covered in our discussion of the first three foundations—have significantly influenced our behavior. Inner thought doesn't choose how we act, so much as it narrates the events, asserting a false sense of self-control. In an oft-employed analogy by neuroscientists, thought is like a monkey riding on the head of an elephant, which represents all the unconscious, implicit processes of the brain. The monkey frantically shouts at the elephant, believing it is controlling the latter's movements, but the elephant (the unconscious mind) is really calling the shots. The monkey simply tells a story, much like our inner chatter.

This is why it's so difficult to change core behaviors, such as trying to talk oneself down from a panic attack, or trying to be more confident in social settings, only to once again shut down. Thoughts fail to control addictions, ingrained habits, reactions, emotional outbursts, anxiety-based procrastination, and so on because they arrive last in the causal chain of influences.

This is why the Buddha cleverly placed awareness of our interpretations of the world last in the foundations of mindfulness; his system inverts how we generally relate to our internal experience. We try to think and define and explain our way through life, but our interpretations of the world are imprecise and often ineffectual.

So let's conclude this chapter where we started: How to

decide whether or not to accept an opportunity? As I read the email containing the offer to teach, I stay present with the experience, and turn my attention to how I'm breathing, whether the breaths are long or short—long indicating ease, shallow indicating agitation. I note the areas where gut feelings express core reactions such as fear or eagerness—the former conveyed via taut, contracted muscles of the abdomen, chest, throat, and shoulders; the latter expressed via relaxed, easeful states in the same places. I take into account the nonverbal moods expressed, such as the settled, calm, and spacious state of attention, which expresses acceptance and confidence, or the jumpy and cramped state of mind associated with anxiety and vulnerability. Finally, I consider whether my jaw is tight or relaxed, as well as the micro-muscles around my eyes and forehead, which so often signal recognizable emotional concerns. Only then do I make any attempt to "figure out what's best" via the mind's narrative capabilities.

The practice just described may take all of thirty seconds or as long as twenty minutes, depending on how much time is available to respond. Yet no matter how short the practice, I can promise the reader, after years of firsthand experience, that taking into account one's breath, gut feelings, and moods invariably provides access to greater experience and wisdom. When we listen to all the body tries to communicate, rather than turning a deaf ear, we encounter new sources of guidance.

7. LOOKING INTO THE ABYSS

WHEN WE FACE UP to the emptiness and disconnection that a superficial life brings, the path really begins.

People celebrate birth all over the world. We celebrate as the family grows, legacies extend, and life endures. It is a time of joy. With each new arrival we may even sense that we belong to something enduring, which may instill a sense of place or purpose in our world.

But the joy of birth conceals a fundamental truth: Life is not easy. Birth results in aging, sickness, loss, and eventual death. Our traditions that celebrate life contrast with the ways we hide the darker things that life entails. We tuck away the sick in hospitals, send the old to retirement, and trolley the dead to morgues. Even the grieving are encouraged to compartmentalize their sorrows in therapeutic settings, safely out of sight. Given the taboos around aging, sickness, deprivation, and death, we may actually feel a sense of shame as we go through one of the challenging transitions of life. But no matter how we hide it from public view, life is not easy and much of it seems meaningless.

We can, however, struggle to find a reason to persevere despite our losses and heartaches. Such inquiries are the bedrock of spiritual practice. The very harsh nature of existence itself demands that I constantly investigate my priorities, putting aside any commitments that fail to bring about spiritual growth or meaningful connection with others.

The modern world's relentless modernization can rob us of a sense of purpose, stripping away our higher values and beliefs. Where do we seek lasting value amid the routines of waking, grooming, eating, working, paying bills, and so forth? Without the supervision of spiritual reflection, my priorities can easily skew toward accomplishing ephemeral, ultimately hollow tasks.

Addiction and Denial

As survival becomes frantic and peace increasingly rare, we may begin to doubt that life really has any purpose. We may assert the importance of our empty routines and vapid pursuits, refusing to seek what lies beyond the busyness of our everyday reality. Rather than searching through the pain for purpose, we may just search for a way out of the pain.

To avoid feelings of emptiness and discontent that come when we glimpse this truth, we turn to habits, hobbies, distractions—drink, drugs, shopping, eating, working, chasing sex. To keep ourselves on the beaten path, we minimize our feelings of unhappiness and rationalize away our disenchantment with cognitive distortions, such as "It's not easy for any-one." Putting on a brave face, we tell ourselves it's all right, rather than admitting that the life we're living is unsatisfying.

Addiction, in particular, is often an attempt to self-repair emotional wounds resulting from early relationships—especially those with caretakers—that failed to address our core needs. If, as children, we express states such as fear, anger, sadness, loneliness, frustration, or confusion to adults who are incapable of tolerant, friendly, nurturing responses, we will quickly learn to repress our negative emotions at all costs. In teenage years, we'll deal with the various emotions and impulses, often sexual, that our caretakers couldn't handle via the self-numbing of substances and addictive behaviors.

Meanwhile, to survive our family systems, we may learn to construct a false self: the caretaker, the people pleaser, the perfectionist, the striver, the ever-enthusiastic, upbeat partic-ipant. Given the difficulties that we see in the world—starva-tion, disease, poverty—admitting we are unhappy may result in a flurry of guilt-inducing doubt. Who am I to complain? Who am I to be unhappy? When asked how we are doing, we respond, "Everything's fine." The pressures to socially conform and comply keep us from looking into the abyss.

We might even project our discontent onto others—it's so-and-so who's ungrateful and unhappy, not I. Disingen-uous though it is, it is another way to keep unsafe feelings at bay.

In one manner or another, we stay in step and keep our-selves moving in order to keep from thinking too much about our ultimate dissatisfaction. This is too bad—that dissatisfaction offers us the opportunity to broaden our perspective. A fundamentally disappointing experience can shake us from the ceaseless pursuit of happiness and security via financial gain and sensual pleasure. This is why the Buddha elevates seemingly negative experiences to the level of great insights: The path requires disenchantment with life as usual, along with a sense of dismay, or even shame, over our values, and a consequent sense of spiritual urgency, a desire to escape this trap. It's when we become tired of it all that we have our opening; dissatisfaction offers us an opportunity to seek out what is missing.

We don't wander into spiritual communities hoping to find peace when everything's okay. We generally wait until we're mired in stress and suffering before asking, "Is continuing this way really worth it?" The most useful and spiritually important things that ever happened to me were my darkest stages of clinical depression. Falling apart that way forced me out of the comfortable but ultimately delusional trance of work, consume, sleep, repeat until death.

When pressed by life, we ask ourselves, "Will this matter? Will this really make me happy? When I'm dying will this help me define my life?"

Looking into the Mind

So how do we open our eyes to the hollowness of life? We look into our own minds.

We may think that we already see our mental habits, as we

encounter them every day. But in Buddhist forms of contemplation, we engage our thoughts from a different perspective. They are observed from the outside; they're no longer considered ours but like an array of mirrors that distort and flatten the world. In daily life our minds can tell us that we are failures, and we believe it without much hesitation. But once we've achieved even the slightest detachment, such thoughts are experienced as ludicrous.

Distance is acquired by keeping the breath and body in mind and welcoming each new thought. If we welcome something, we cannot think of it as ours, so the very act of greeting establishes distance. Greeting thoughts also curtails resistance, which is the fountainhead of stress. It may seem contradictory, but what we do not refuse or defend against in the mind will not overwhelm us. We are only engulfed by that which we continually resist.

When we are detached, we relate to even the most catastrophizing thoughts with healthy suspicion. It's like analyzing a salesperson's pitch without purchasing their wares—noting the techniques of peddling, how slogans are repeated, the unlikely promises and assurances employed to gain our trust. My thoughts really want me to believe they're both mine and real, but they're neither.

So where can I find transcendent meaning, if not in language-based cognitive thoughts? The quest for truth is not found in the conceptual realm, but in the experiential. With some patient, sustained attention to our inner experience, especially the space between thoughts and the sensations that go on beneath them, we can let go of those things that distract us from the fundamental experience of being: external interruptions—only a smartphone or laptop away—the challenges of relationships and careers, and the various conflicts that arise from stress beneath the surface. As we start to let go of our preoccupations, time seems to slow down. When we no longer dismiss the present moment as a period of time we need to get through to get somewhere else, we can open to a vast, fluid realm of sensations, a constant stream that presents itself for receptive observation. If we let go of our habitual tendencies to criticize, comment, and weave it all into a story, our over-reliance upon conceptual thought is challenged.

The true wisdom of life often arises in the gaps between thoughts. This inner investigation isn't easy to begin, much less maintain. Such indwelling can feel vulnerable, or even dangerous. And once our distracting stories have been put aside, there's the tendency to reinstate other misleading stories. We could replace the story about the importance of our career with another about how spiritual we are.

As a skillful substitute for thought-based mental content, the great Ajahn Sumedho suggested returning to the suitably empty, unbiased thought "just this."

I'll give you an example: I have a tendency to suppress uncomfortable moods and feelings. When I'm experiencing loneliness, I'll feel the urge to switch on the television or snack on Corn Nuts, since binge eating creates the sense of being taken care of, alleviating the feelings of isolation. When I'm frustrated by a colleague not returning an email,

I'll gravitate toward shopping online, rather than simply feeling the disappointment. Then, months later, the repressed emotion returns and seeks an outlet—I might find myself suddenly short-tempered with my wife, for instance.

So I try to push away discomfort, rather than turning toward challenging emotions as they arise and assimilating them into my human experience. Suppression doesn't process anything; it simply puts off the inevitable obligation to experience our full range of emotions. If we push agitating states away from us, refusing to acknowledge and tend to them, we abandon ourselves; a sense of emptiness, hollowness, can be felt. In "Just this" practice, on the other hand, we allow ourselves to feel whatever emotional state has arisen and presented itself to the body and mind. All the really unpleasant moments of life we turn to and reclaim. Envy? Just envy. Boredom? Just boredom.

Returning again and again to this receptive awareness offers a foundation upon which we can build an authentic life. It allows us to see meaning appearing briefly behind the constant parade of thoughts and images. It takes a good deal of patience and repetitive endeavor, but it's there for everyone. In meditation we find that there is nothing to acquire or defeat, nothing to defend or protect. We return to "just this."

While experience unfolds, awareness remains—detached, unblemished, transcendent. Slowing down my mind, relaxing the breath, and increasing the space between thoughts provides me with distance from the mundane, which in turn provides a transcendent reality.

Practice:
Returning to the Emotional Body

Settle into a comfortable posture, head balanced above the shoulders—the only effort we need is to keep the head or shoulders from slouching over the chest. Breathe in an unaffected rhythm.

Bring to mind a recent, unpleasant event from daily life: for example, a tense interaction with a friend or family member, or a long time on hold waiting to speak with customer service representative.

Now, bring awareness to the areas in the body where somatic sensations of emotions are generally felt: the muscles of the abdomen, chest, throat, and face.

Notice any muscle contractions in this region, no matter how subtle or muted they appear. It's not important to discern which affect you are experiencing, nor is it useful to analyze why the experience is occurring. The goal is to know that an emotion is present and to be with it, rather than turning to external distractions (television, internet, and so forth).

Having located the emotion in the body, it's time to become familiar with its expressive components: do we feel it as throbbing waves of contraction, hollowness, a tight grip, suffocating, or burning? If the sensations feel overpowering, relax the muscles in the surrounding areas, such as the shoulders, arms, buttocks, legs.

Each time an emotion is detected, explore the sensations as thoroughly as possible; the more meticulous we are, the sooner the feelings will pass. Emotions are messages from the unconscious informing us that an important interpersonal event has occurred; once they're felt and acknowledged, much of their work is done and they start to recede.

If an emotional activation doesn't pass, when the meditation has concluded, seek out a receptive friend and talk about the experience. Sometimes activations not only seek our attention but the attention of others, so that we can restore a sense of connectedness to our lives.

This practice need not take longer than five minutes and can be accomplished as an interlude during a breath meditation; once completed we return to the breath and use it to relax the areas where emotions were experienced.

8. OUR PERSONAL EMOTIONAL HISTORY

WITH A LITTLE REFLECTION, we find that much of our habitual behavior is an attempt to get rid of unpleasant feelings or to divert our attention from them in other ways. We chase pleasure, substances, or distraction via Facebooking, texting, shopping, gaming—anything to push away the stress.

Of course it would make more sense to tackle our deeper problems so that we can alleviate our long-term suffering. So why do we instead habitually avoid what's really going on with us? Buddhist thinking tells us that it is not a simple procrastination, but a cycle of inclination, feeling, and craving.

Early experience creates underlying moods and inclinations (*namarupa*, in Pali) for the way we relate to our bodies. One could think of the namarupa as a kind of proto-personality, a realm of impulses. As we stumble across various situations and experiences, given our own namarupa, feelings (*vedana*) of comfort and discomfort appear. For example, because of my own namarupa, if I find myself alone at a gathering, I may feel insecurity, first as tension in my abdomen, chest, and shoulders, which makes me start gulping air. This is how my insecurity manifests. If on the other hand, I meet someone and we connect, I'll feel relaxation in those same places and my breath will be deep and smooth.

Our namarupa may develop inclinations to seek or avoid certain feelings, which leads to craving (*tanhā*) to get rid of what feels uncomfortable and cling to what feels good. In my example above, in order to avoid the discomfort of my insecurity, I might crave to speak to someone immediately or to have social media on my phone distract me. Or I could avoid the discomfort by avoiding gatherings altogether. In any case my craving is to avoid the discomfort and/or seek some other comfort.

With a little reason and reflection, it is easy to see how this applies to each of us. What are some things that we seek or avoid? What are the feelings we experience that inspire us to seek or avoid them? What are the underlying moods and inclinations behind those feelings?

A Lifetime's History of Anxiety

The Natural Anxiety of Vulnerability

The earliest form of anxiety is the anxiety of vulnerability— some call it "annihilation anxiety." As infants we're helpless, incapable of defending ourselves against anything. We're in a large world with very little control over our own bodies or movements, so we feel a sense of vulnerability to the world. Our parents help us to establish a sense of security by lifting us up and cradling us, giving us a sense of security. Someone is watching over us.

The connection that relieves this anxiety arrives through touch, glance, movement, because we are yet too young to understand words. When someone holds, caresses, and soothes us with soft facial expressions and cooing tones of voice, a felt sense of security appears. All of these nonverbal messages and caretaking behaviors provide the first powerful feelings of being safe in the world; a wellspring of positive emotions arise from feeling connected.

Separation Anxiety

Eventually we acquire language and our parents reassure us verbally, but our parents are not always there. As infants we can feel that insecurity any time our parents are out of view: for example, every time we wake up alone. As toddlers we might feel this if we find ourselves lost in a store or are first left at kindergarten. If we actually lost a parent during childhood, say to death or divorce, this feeling will be even more intense and long lasting. The negative feelings of loneliness and sadness that build up around feeling disconnected become separation anxiety.

As children, when we expect a separation might happen, we will deal with it in a couple of different ways. One is that we resort to protest behaviors—flop to the ground, kick, and scream until someone heeds us, or until we wear ourselves out. Or we might retreat into the realm of imagination, fabricating a distracting reality to suppress the feelings of insecurity and isolation.

Later in life these manifest as two different ways to relate to anxiety triggers. On the one hand, we can act out by expressing the anxiety. We do this in order to avoid or manipulate the world around us, to keep the dreaded experience from happening. On the other hand, we can repress our feelings: unconsciously try to keep the experience itself at a distance by retreating into the mind, away from the body where we feel the contractions of vulnerability. The feelings of separation are overwhelming and painful. In either case we unconsciously react to threat of abandonment.

Neurotic Anxiety

Neurotic anxiety is the concern that we will act on an impulse that will make the world—everyone else—reject us. As our attention turns from ourselves to the rest of the world, our anxiety conversely shifts from worrying about the uncertainty of the world to the uncertainty of ourselves. This anxiety develops as we start to socialize; we worry that an unconscious impulse will assume control of our actions, resulting in embarrassing behaviors.

So our personal development of anxiety has progressed from unease over what might be out *there* to an apprehension over what might be in *here*; our own urges and impulses. The mistrust has turned against us: the danger might actually lurk within us.

When we are children and we cry loudly from fear, spill food in frustration, gesture angrily, and a stressed caretaker becomes exasperated, our "secure base"—the safe space to express our needs—dissolves. We begin to see that some of our own impulses and urges lead to abandonment. So when we begin to socialize in school, where it seems that the other kids know each other and have been given the "How to Be Cool" rulebook that we seem to have missed, we worry that our awkward, bumbling attempts to connect will result in ridicule and rejection. We begin to mistrust our own inclinations and emotions. What arises from us may apparently result in rejection, ostracism, and desertion.

In adolescence, once again, we defend ourselves by acting out—lashing out with hostility or contempt—or by retreating into the many fantasy lives available to young people: TV, movies, comic books. The realm of fantasy becomes less appealing, however, as we enter our teen years and adult life. We naturally develop different ways to cope with anxiety, but our new methods can still be sorted into those same two categories: (1) ways of seeking shelter in our minds, or defense mechanisms, and (2) ways of manipulating the world around us, or acting out.

Defense mechanisms can be less apparent to us than our ways of acting out, so I'll give some examples here.

Defense Mechanisms

Intellectualization

Intellectualization involves focusing on *solving* the issue, rather than attending to the feeling of the experience. Too often, our thoughts provide a false refuge, an escape hatch from what's happening: an unending stream of thoughts to distract us from what's really going on. The Buddha called this *ditthi upadana*, clinging to views and opinions as a form of resistance to experience.

Catastrophizing

Catastrophizing is visualizing the worst outcome of any situation. It's a variation of intellectualization, in that it distracts us from the underlying emotional experience with that old core feeling of believing the world doesn't love us. Any kind of scarcity—a lack of work, friendship, sex—efficiently activates our fear of loneliness. We don't want to feel lonely, so we might instead consider all of the worst things that can happen. If we don't have work, for example, we can imagine all of the ways that we will go broke. If we are without friends or lovers, we can imagine all of the ways that we will die alone.

It begs the question: Why would we prefer all of these nightmarish realities to the feeling of loneliness itself? Catastrophizing stories are alluring; they make us feel prepared. They can even provide a false sense of security: as if, since we have considered the worst, it won't happen. But its most obvious effect is concealing the embodied emotional experience.

Avoidance Coping

Avoidance coping is the tendency to simply avoid those things that make us uncomfortable. Phobias are a very common example of this. Almost everyone has something that gives them anxiety. Very common ones include a fear of heights, public speaking, etc. In these two particular examples, the anxiety is often not produced by the threat of something else coming to do harm to the person, but rather by the fact that we might betray ourselves. Many people feel anxiety around ledges. It's not often that they are worried about being pushed, so much as they feel a strange impulse to leap. Likewise, most people who imagine speaking in front of a crowd don't imagine being overtly rejected but simply imagine that they will do something embarrassing.

In these two examples, though, one might catastrophize as described above, imagining the worst-case scenarios. But, given how uncomfortable that is, why not just avoid those situations altogether? If I am uncomfortable near ledges, I'll just stay away from them. If I might be embarrassed at social functions, I'll just stay home. Avoid all the bad thoughts as well as the bad feelings. In the end, I may end up avoiding my community, or sources of help, as well.

The Results of Anxiety-Based Repression

Eventually our anxieties can instill defense mechanisms that are too efficient, keeping us unaware of a wide array of important emotional information. Our ability to function mentally or socially might be hindered by discomfort we feel beneath the surface, for example.

We need to rely on far more than logic or reason if we're to navigate the complex arenas of interpersonal life. We constantly rely on embodied feeling-states—our guts, so to speak—in order to make wise decisions in critical situations. When we are really good at something, we often rely on intuition, which is another word for an emotional response. People who cannot read the emotional body become incapable of making wise judgments. We cannot survive without our full emotional palettes.

The question may be asked "When is it safe to follow our intuition, and when should we override our gut feelings and seek external guidance?"

A basic rule of thumb practice would be as follows: *We should trust our instincts only in arenas wherein we've developed a significant degree of solid experience.* For example, if an interior decorator is asked what color a room should be painted, they need not ponder the physics of color or solve the issue intellectually; their years of training and discernment, stored in largely unconscious memory storage, will use the fast circuits of the mind to provide a quick response. On the other hand, in arenas in which we have little acquaintanceship, we should learn to seek other people's insights before fully trusting our intuition. For example, when traveling to unknown cities and locations, following instincts could easily lead one into unsafe or thoroughly disappointing neighborhoods; this is why wise travelers consult either travel guide books or trustworthy local residents for suggestions.

Furthermore, in relationships, if we have either anxious or avoidant tendencies, then we should learn to override our intuition—which is telling us to worry or run away—and turn instead toward the challenging tasks of stating our needs aloud. In this case, happiness will be found where our gut instincts won't lead us: with secure partners who do not run when we seek intimacy.

Still, according to neuroscientists such as Antonio Damasio, we cannot be rational without considering our emotional, gut reactions to situations. Scientists have demonstrated that we constantly rely on physical feelings of intuition in order to make wise decisions in critical situations. People who cannot read the emotional body by interpreting their physical feelings—perhaps due to damage to certain parts of their brains, substance addiction, or self-numbing tendencies—are incapable of sound judgment; they flounder and become indecisive to the point of confusion and despair.

Our most painful feelings—sadness, despair, loneliness, and frustration—contain crucial information. For example, they can let us know when we're disconnected from support or in partnerships that are no longer satisfactory. There are many individuals who'll stay in loveless, empty relationships, as they can see no sense in seeking a deeper happiness with another. It is deceptively easier to repress the recognition that there's something fundamentally wrong with our priorities. It is deceptively easier simply to keep ourselves blind to needs we've failed to address, and ultimately, to live without integrity.

Emotions also constantly prime us to take action. We can mask an emotion, replacing an unsafe experience, such as fear, with one that feels more secure, such as aggression. We can minimize our feelings, by telling ourselves and others that we're not really hurt. We can take drugs to alleviate the emotion altogether.

But our impulses don't simply vanish because they're inconvenient to the rational, narrative mind. No matter how efficiently we repress our emotions by focusing on our inner chatter—which effectively deflects our attention from the body and the unconscious messages it conveys—their driving forces remain locked and loaded waiting to express themselves. Repressed feelings will rise up from the shadows whenever a present situation in any resembles a previously wounding experience, at which point fear, anger, sadness, guilt, embarrassment once again return, reappearing in tidal waves of pent-up energy, utterly unregulated, flowing energies too strong for others to handle.

No one can indefinitely repress the authentic, spontaneous, and true impulses, memories, and feelings that render us whole. Repression strips us of our dynamic experience, leaving us squeezed into tidy boxes that may look good on the outside, but are internally suffocating. The more authentic energies we bury, the greater the sense of being hollow inside, for that is what we're doing: emptying ourselves of that which animates life. Reliance on narratives, intellectualization, and catastrophizing simply delays underlying unease rather than teaching us how to simply be with those core feelings.

The View from the Dharma

The Dharma presents the same core observation as modern psychology: the mind is capable of hosting and pursuing entirely incompatible agendas. Anxiety, panic, dissociation, and sudden outbursts are messages from the unconscious mind, informing us that it's terrified or enraged.

During such bouts of anxiety and emotional disruption,

internal awareness provides the most useful tool for recognition and regulation of emotions. *Sati*, or inner awareness, is a practice in which we prevent the mind from wandering away with thoughts, observing all the embodied sensations and moods that underlie our present experience. This can be accomplished alone with eyes closed, or in a business meeting or crowded subway car with eyes open. It's a liberating practice, in that when we learn to detach from the inner chatter and mental movies that so easily captivate our attention, we can return home to the body, which is the gateway to self-integration; at last, the intellectual and emotional can become aware of each other and begin the process of healing, rather than relying on anxiety to signal we're not of one mind.

Turning to our emotions can feel like a strange practice, as we live in a hectic, materialist culture that encourages us to achieve and accumulate rather than attend to difficult emotional activations such as anxiety. When internal stresses become too great, and they result in anxiety or panic, we're encouraged to medicate—which can provide some help, but is never the entire solution. If we want to heal and live authentic, meaningful lives, we should view our agitation as important messages worth reading rather than suppressing, repressing, or all-too-quickly medicating them away. In essence, anxiety is a challenge, an invitation to become whole: will we answer it or keep running away?

Practice: *AIM*

For working with anxiety I'd like to recommend a simple practice called AIM, which is an acronym for *Accept, Inquire*, and *Mother*.

The *A* for *acceptance* involves the open, receptive recognition that a strong emotion is present. All this requires is turning toward what's present, rather than resisting. I like the phrase "I see you, Mara!" as a tool to aid in this process. You see, the Buddha had a shadow-self called Mara, a representation of all the sensual urges and indulgences he put aside to pursue the path to enlightenment. Of course the Buddha's repressed urges didn't go away quietly, so Mara would arise now and then, urging him to abandon his difficult spiritual journey and return to material splendor. Unlike Jesus, who commanded his devil away, the Buddha would respond with, "I see you, Mara," in essence acknowledging rather than repressing or indulging those urges.

Let me provide an example: Fifteen years or so ago, I went on a sober retreat to an island in the Caribbean, a vacation for which I had been amassing funds for some time. Also attending the spiritual retreat, and staying in the same hotel, was a very loud and boorish private group. They ignored every instruction and request from the retreat's staff, cut in food lines with the greatest entitlement, chatted loudly during times set aside for meditation and yoga, and so forth. I reached a point where simply stumbling upon any one of them—and they were everywhere—would trigger fury, which in turn would encourage my mind to engage in endless inner speeches about rudeness and how certain people are better off as meals for sharks. The solution was to think, "I see you, Mara" as I encountered each of these tiresome individuals. The practice reminded me to accept their presence and turn, instead, to what I was experiencing internally, rather than engage upon another endless inner speech about manners and the like.

The *I* in AIM stands for *inquire*, means pulling attention away from thoughts or external dramas and paying attention to what's occurring in the body, gut feelings, even the energy levels of the mind. Inquiring or investigating emotions requires creating a "safe container," a body that can relax around the activations. So, for example, if my anxiety expresses itself via a tight abdomen, I can relax the muscles of the arms and legs, release the shoulders, open the chest, breath comfortably. The less tension I feel elsewhere in the body, the easier it will be to hold the principal activation.

The *M* for *mother* reminds us to nurture what's present, to soothe the agitation. After all, most of my fears were ingrained when I was very young, when I didn't have the skills that are available to me now. Today I can survive the conflicts, rejections, setbacks, and frustrations that would have left me distraught as a child, but my fear doesn't know that unless I take the time to gently reassure these emotions. So I'll use a simple phrase, such as, "I care about you, I'll take care of you," and repeat the words, slowly and calmly, in the mind while I focus on the body. While the emotional mind struggles with words and ideas, as it is largely located in the brain's right hemisphere, which doesn't have the language centers of the left hemisphere, it understands moods, feelings, images. By repeating a soft, simple phrase such as "It will be okay" in the same comforting tone one would speak to an agitated child, we can "speak to" emotional circuits and slowly deactivate them.

This practice helps me stay with emotional states as they present themselves, while cultivating a deeper understanding of what underlies or fuels my anxiety. I offer it has a way to approach agitation, a way to transform the upheaval into a revealing experience that can be held and safely expressed.

9. MAKING ROOM FOR DIFFICULT PASSENGERS

WE FLEE THE DISCOMFORT of difficult emotions, which we experience in the body, toward the shelter of the mind, but we need to stop abandoning ourselves and make room for all experiences, not only those that are easy and light.

While we cannot deny the infinite usefulness of the human mind, some of its processes do not benefit us so much. One of these is repression: the way that we tamp down our most uncomfortable memories, impulses, and emotions, keeping them out of our consciousness. We can keep at bay the feelings of grief and despair of traumatic losses, the loneliness of isolation, the anger resulting from insults and harm. We can restrain impulses that are not tolerated by those around us, even if they are critical to our identity, gender, sexuality. Indeed, we can suppress our most natural and authentic instincts, if we think they might jeopardize our relationship to our peers. Humans are social animals. We survive by bonding, and separation feels like a very real threat to our well-being. As a result, our family and peers exert an overwhelming influence on the development of our personality, to the point that we construct entire identities, to meet the single, overriding demand of finding love.

Of course casting out our painful experiences ultimately spares us nothing, because what we suppress doesn't simply evaporate or go away. The emotions and impulses are stored in an unconscious well of physical discomfort and emotional pain, what Jung refers to as the *shadow*. This is the realm of the repressed.

The tendency to exclude the unwanted from awareness comes at a significant cost to our overall well-being and lasting happiness. We are meant to feel our full range of emotions and impulses, even when they're harmful. The safest process is to *hold* our negative feelings—aggression, fear, sorrow—without either acting out or suppressing. By creating a safe container for our unwanted emotions, we can live fuller, more genuine, emotionally healthy lives.

Those painful experiences continue to exert their influence and take their toll, whether we attend to them or not. However, defense mechanisms only work until they don't. After a great deal of our energy is expended on this lost cause, anxiety rises up, letting us know our defenses are down and that the repressed is returning with a vengeance. Soon the smiles we plaster on, along with the business demeanor, fades, and the anxiety stage of barely holding it all together comes along. Eventually the narratives we think and tell about ourselves begin to crumble, as they no longer adequately "tell the story" of our lives.

The identity stories that we construct to get love and success in the world are always simplifications. By telling the story of our more admirable traits—that we are caring, clever, creative, witty, etc.—we have to exclude our less appealing ones—that we are also insecure, lost, and overwhelmed. To win security in a world of abandonment, we are pressured into presenting a story of ourselves that doesn't really reflect who we are, but rather what other people can believe. Over the years, if we're not careful, the distance will grow between our narratives and our natural spontaneous, feelings.

Again: these personal narratives—even the ones we only tell ourselves—are established not to reflect the truth of who we are and what we feel, but simply to get love. Theoretically if we feel securely connected in childhood, the narratives that we create and show the world will be close enough to our authentic feelings that we'll be able to sustain the story for our entire lives. But if the distance becomes too great between the story and the felt truth, the result will be anxiety and despair.

Defense Mechanisms

We have a lot of defense mechanisms at work in us, keeping these feelings buried as deeply as possible. These defense mechanisms deny, distort, and keep this content out of awareness. A lot of our defense mechanisms work simply by keeping us unaware of our bodies, where our core emotions express themselves, so that we can feel safer. What follows are some examples of common defense mechanisms.

Busyness/Workaholism

The most socially rewarded defense mechanism in this country is busyness or workaholism. But busyness is just a ploy to keep us from feeling our feelings. When we stop and feel, suddenly they all rush back into us, and the experience is overpowering, frightening. No wonder we keep ourselves so busy. Hardly anybody really loves their work so much that they would gleefully do it for sixty hours per week. We might claim that we do. But if we stop that work long enough, the feelings come flooding back to us along with the terror of feeling them. This lets us know that our work was less a labor of love and more an avoidance coping scheme. If we stay busy, we don't have to feel all the pain of what we have repressed in the shadows.

Projection

Another way we might deny the presence of feelings we don't like is by projecting them onto other people. For example, people who are uncomfortable with their anger may see other people as very angry, or hostile toward them. People who are struggling with their sexuality may look at other people and project their impulses onto them. By projecting our feelings out onto other people, we do not have to feel the discomfort of how disappointed we are with ourselves.

Masking Emotions

We also use some emotions to mask others that are harder to face. Jealousy and envy are often used to cover up deeper grief from life-long wounds. Similarly distress is often masked by more assertive feelings like anger, which deflects us away from feeling vulnerable.

Suppose we want to quit our current job and find something more meaningful. If this is so daunting that we don't even take the first steps to do it, the anxiety and dissatisfaction can press us to bring out a completely different emotion. We might convey to others that we really love the job and never want to leave. But somewhere below that, we know the truth and can't puzzle out why we would say something so untrue.

Humor and Minimizing

In order to escape the discomfort of our more difficult emotions, we may deny that the feelings are painful or important by rationalizing that whatever is causing the pain is much less significant than it is. Suppose, for example, we were bullied in our school years, repeatedly pushed, tripped, insulted, verbally humiliated in front of others. If we felt the abuse was too painful to hold, when our parents asked "What's wrong?" we may have chosen to downplay the events, claiming we were simply teased or the victim of a harmless prank. We diminish the pain to avoid activating the emotional content—fear, anger, embarrassment—we've suppressed. Minimizing cuts off entirely healthy and natural emotional responses to painful life events; it transforms the scary or traumatic into simplistic, coldly rational stories, to avoid having to feel what's been repressed. It is just another way that we seek refuge in thinking as a way to block painful feelings.

In my family there was a strong tendency to make light of

anything associated with guilt. I remember once expressing disappointment that my mother forgot our plans to see the movie *Apocalypse Now* in its opening week. She responded, with an exaggerated, put-upon voice, "You're right! I'm the worst mother ever": her go-to response to avoid apologizing for mistakes. I certainly have this tendency as well, making light of times I've acted inappropriately as a way to circumvent the feelings of shame; on other occasions I'll dismiss acknowledging the wounds others have caused, laughing off the harsh remarks. Humor, when over-relied upon, conceals important energies that express disappointment or shame; it denies the emotional reactions that allow us to feel and address our wounds. Of course, there are those who will retort that humor can be an adult, skillful coping strategy. It is possible that the capability to laugh makes it likelier we'll be able to reflect and discuss traumatic events, in future settings, without dissociation (disconnecting from present time events) or hypervigilance (feeling vulnerable to attack while in safe settings, looking out for nonexistent threats.) Unfortunately, humor tends to create the perception we're all right, presenting the appearance that things aren't as difficult as they really are. If we depend on it too much, others aren't cued to help us articulate our pain.

Working with Anger

I've found it difficult to make any headway on the Buddhist path without encountering and working with difficult, agitating emotions—sadness, disgust, fear, and especially anger.

Anger is an agitated state of mind that can easily lead to hatred and violence if unchecked. Yet I don't believe it's possible to *get rid* of anger; it is a universal emotion deeply rooted in ingrained survival reactions. My goal is to *live* with anger—as well as other difficult emotions—in a skillful way so that it doesn't cause harm.

How do I practice with anger in order to achieve that?

There are many types of anger. For example, there's the anger I feel after watching or reading about social injustice. The energy of this type of anger can be helpful. Taking action requires experiencing enough outrage that I'm compelled to volunteer, protest, or support the causes that address social injustice—without allowing my indignation to erupt into violence.

Another type of anger is made up of grudges that camouflage grief. I mentor many people who carry around unending resentments at those who've abandoned them, whether lovers, spouses, partners, parents, or family members. What I find is that harboring such resentment creates the illusion that we can protect ourselves from ever being abandoned again.

Our underlying belief is that if we replay the events often enough in our minds, we'll be safe. But believe me, it's very possible to be wounded by others while being filled with resentments—that was the gist of my twenty years of alcohol dependence. As the son of an alcoholic father, I lived with my share of bitterness, which only blocked me from processing the deeper emotions of grief and sadness that needed care and attention. Fortunately I learned to work past the "unfairness of it all" through Buddhist therapy and insight meditation practice, in which I practiced recognizing the deeper, more painful, emotions.

Then there is the type of anger that erupts when we experience small indignities in daily life. Here are two examples of situations like that in which I failed, at first, to process anger in a skillful way.

A little while ago, I was riding my bike over the Williamsburg Bridge. There was only one person ahead of me on the Brooklyn-bound bike lane, and he was a good distance ahead. At one point I looked away from the path, and in the time it took for me to do so, he had gotten off his bike and put it down in a way that completely blocked the path.

He was now less than ten feet away me. I screeched to a stop and inadvertently yelled "Damn!" (which in Brooklynese is like saying a friendly hello). Maybe I gave him a quizzical look as I pedaled past, but nothing more. A moment later he yelled out in my direction, in the most sarcastic voice you can imagine, "I'm sorry if I ruined your night . . .. *asshole!*"

I continued over the bridge in an agitated state—my shoulders almost touching my ears, my jaw locked, my thoughts caught in a self-righteous spiral. You see, when I experience some form of poor treatment, my mind provides, free of charge, an inner lawyer who delivers long speeches about how horrible the world is today, everything's only getting worse, *blah blah blah*.

Then the revenge fantasies started up, with the creation of a series of perfect retorts in which I visualized myself riding back and yelling at my night-ruiner. Then I heard yet another inner lawyer—this time apparently a Buddhist—argue back: "You should be above all this. You just taught a meditation class! Clearly, you're doing your practice all wrong . . ." So my mind ping-ponged back and forth between "I'm going to tell that guy what's what," and "I shouldn't be feeling this angry."

Anger, though, doesn't pay attention to any such *shoulds*. Anger and other emotions like fear are core survival impulses, and they will never be displaced by logic or reason or being told to just go away. Such inner speeches are decoys, false refuges that keep us from feeling the actual, physical sensations of our emotions.

The experience of anger is difficult to sit with, and it can feel easier and safer to retreat into our heads and listen as our thoughts prattle on about the unfairness of life. But as I can attest, our resentments don't alleviate our anger. After spending my childhood with a drunk, violent father, I carried outraged victimization stories around for years. All they did was continually reactivate my rage rather than relieve it.

Let's look at another example of poor emotion regulation. A few years back, I got a call from my bank: "Hello, Mr. Korda. We recently had a teller who revealed customers' PIN numbers to a known felon. Funds were subsequently emptied out of some accounts, and yours was involved. We're going to send you a form that you should fill out, and then wait to get your money back. And we recommend that you purchase our identity-fraud protection plan."

I became furious and laid into this poor bank employee. But in addition to being unpleasant, my reaction was a complete waste of time and energy. All I needed to do was ask to speak to a supervisor. I eventually did, and got everything sorted. My temper tantrum hadn't relieved any stress. Instead, I walked around furious for days afterward, feeling mistreated. And the decision to call and offer the identify-fraud program hadn't been the bank employee's choice—she was simply following protocol. All that my venting provided was an illusion that I could externalize and thereby relieve my anger.

But it doesn't work that way. As the psychologist Jeffrey Lohr recently concluded after a meta-analysis of a wide variety of clinical studies, "Expressing anger does not reduce aggressive tendencies and likely makes it worse." In other words, when I'm venting I'm trying to externalize—to push outside of myself and onto someone else—feelings that are meant to be felt in my body.

Over the last decade of mentoring, not to mention my years in Buddhist therapy, I've learned that emotions are alleviated in only a couple of ways:

(1) *By being felt.* Emotions seek our attention by creating physical sensations—the tight abdomen or chest, the pounding heartbeat, the contraction of throat muscles, facial expressions, shaking limbs, etc.—for us to feel. Emotions speak via the body, while thoughts speak in words.

Emotions are impulses from the unconscious, telling us that an event that affects our survival, or reminds us of an earlier threat or interpersonal disappointment, has occurred. These emotions/impulses also let us know that our subconscious minds have decided that something important has happened, and that we should pay attention to it.

(2) *And by being communicated.* Human beings are social beings. Knowing that others understand what we're experiencing makes us feel less vulnerable.

It's possible to achieve some relief by expressing strong emotions in art, music, dance, writing, and so on, but nothing replaces direct communication: *You're feeling really hurt, wounded, lonely, sad, depressed. I get it. I'm here.* When someone mirrors our emotional state back to us—through words, a knowing smile, or other non-verbal indication—we feel relief. Connection soothes our unconscious survival regions, telling us *You're okay, you're safe, others care about you.* (For more on this, see psychologist Matthew Lieberman's wonderful book, *Social.*)

For many years I relied on alcohol to freeze or get rid of my anger and other feelings. Drinking inhibits awareness of the emotional body where the feelings of anger reside. Others seek out food, shopping, pornography, or other behaviors to distract themselves from the feeling of anger in the body.

Eventually, though, the unacknowledged emotions build and force their way to the surface, and we vent them with even greater force. Have you ever met romantic partners who say they never argue, but then suddenly split apart? When we fail to acknowledge our disappointments and continually bury conflict, eventually huge battles and breakups ensue over minutia like whose turn it was to purchase toilet paper or clean the dishes. Unexpressed and unfelt emotions don't go away; they erupt or eat away at us.

In many of the Buddha's core teachings, he instructed practitioners to do anything they could to replace anger that leads to harmful behavior with skillful alternatives. "Hatred is never allayed by hatred; but only through nonhatred, which is the everlasting way," it says in the *Dhammapada*. Or, "Overcome your anger with the opposite of anger, as you overcome evil with goodness."

This is excellent advice when you might explosively discharge rage or aggression on another being. I find it helps relieve aggressive impulses if I extend my exhalations until they're twice as long as my in-breaths, while also mentally repeating a *metta*, or loving-kindness, phrase to calm my mind, such as "May I feel loved, safe, and at ease." I may also visualize a place where I feel safe, such as a favorite park by the East River.

But if I rely on self-soothing techniques for too long they can turn into what psychologist John Welwood called a "spiritual bypass." That's when I'm using my spiritual practice to suppress my emotions like anger and avoid really addressing them. So I only employ breath, metta, or forgiveness practices to subdue immediate impulses that could lead to harm.

To actually process anger, we have to really face it. It's essential to feel and constructively express the feelings that come with difficult emotions. Look at the Buddha's story of "King Sakka's Demon."

This demon fed on people's resistance and anger. One day the demon climbed onto the king's throne while he was away. Sakka's guards saw the little demon and yelled at it, "How dare you sit on the throne? This is an outrage!" As they yelled, the demon became a ferocious beast, breathing fire and terrifying the guards, who fled.

When King Sakka returned, he tried a different approach. He greeted the demon with kindness. "How can I make you feel comfortable?" he asked. "Can I offer you something to eat? Do you want to put your claws up on the table?" With each nicety, the demon shrank in size. It became smaller and smaller until eventually the king could easily remove it from the throne.

This story is, of course, a metaphor for the way to relate to our anger and other challenging emotions. If we try to get rid, repress, or *should* them, they only get stronger. The real practice is to do what Sakka did: turn toward the anger, make it comfortable, and create a safe place in the body where it can be felt.

When the time comes for communicating anger—which we do in group practices I lead—I find there's no real virtue in a blow-by-blow recollection of past grievances. Little soothing or alleviation occurs when we simply repeat the stories of our woundings, rather than express how we feel about them.

So the most I might say is something like "A teller called

me up; she informed me that thousands of dollars disappeared from my bank account; I yelled at her and now I don't feel too good about that. I still feel angry." Usually, the others will listen with empathy, compassion, and tolerance.

Finally, I'd like to add that all the emotion regulation in the world won't help if we don't develop and stick to adult boundaries when we are in situations wherein harm is continually happening. We should never use spiritual practice as a way to avoid establishing and sticking to rules of conduct in our interpersonal lives.

My father and I spent a decade in family therapy, working to develop a new relationship. He managed to change a great deal, but he never became capable of helping create a safe environment in which I could discuss certain topics—such as my work—without becoming harsh and judgmental. So I had to establish clear boundaries, not only with him, but with myself: *I'm not going to discuss what I'm doing for a living with him, because it's not safe.*

Turning toward the Shadow

It's essential, as a part of our healing journeys, to become aware of what we've repressed as it announces its presence. Fortunately there are a number of signals that indicate an imminent return of the repressed.

When repressed emotions and memories start to arise, they create what's called signal anxiety. Since we only repress what feels threatening or inconvenient, the first sign that something we've pushed down wants our attention will be that we feel distressed and uncomfortable; we'll experience worry, agitation, insomnia, racing thoughts.

When facing the return of repressed mental content, we may return to simplistic coping skills we learned earlier in life. After disappointing setbacks in life, when plans go awry, jobs are lost, businesses fail, new endeavors are dropped, we may hide from our friends, hoping that social withdrawal will spare us from experiencing shame and disappointment; avoidance coping is simply a regressive tendency, one that children employ to hide failures from adults who might heap more shame into the mix. We become incapable, frightened, needy because a fear that we've repressed is making its way back to consciousness.

A more noticeable sign that the repressed is coming back into our awareness is a seeking of intense stimulation: drugs, shopping, gambling, sex, or anything to get away from our feelings. In extreme cases, the reappearance of the repressed may lead to addiction or other compulsive behaviors, as during these stages we often don't feel safe to seek out help. Many times it's only after the behaviors extract far greater tolls—poor choices and personal embarrassments—that we finally turn to ourselves to relate to the shadow self. We find that we need to stop abandoning ourselves and learn to open to all of our experiences, not only what feels light and easy.

Practice:
Understanding Compulsive Behaviors

Compulsions come in many guises—the ritualistic purchase of clothing to reward oneself after a stressful day of work; binging on cookies, candy, or ice cream to combat moods shifting toward sadness or despair; the reactive need to post selfies on social media when loneliness lingers at the edges of awareness. Compulsions are invariably activated by underlying emotions or memories seeking our conscious awareness. The key to understanding and alleviating our addictive routines is to pause and feel into the surfacing emotional content that seeks our attention.

The practice is quite simple. Suppose we feel a daily imperative to consume a donut during the late afternoon hours, as a break from the stresses of the day. The donut, in other words, is a distraction from the agitation of chronic work stress, perhaps even a sugar-coated stimulant to keep us from observing nagging feelings of boredom and purposelessness.

The key is to set a five-minute timer on one's phone or computer, and put off heading out for the donut. As we put off the compulsive routine, what moods do we start to feel? Does the mind become agitated, jumpy, heavy, distracted? Do we feel physically tense? Are we irritable, or suddenly tired and depressed? What thoughts start to appear when the donut is delayed?

Once we can attend to the difficult feelings that lie below our addictive behaviors, we'll find that new choices become possible. If we come to discern that our binge eating is driven by feelings of isolation and disconnection, we can choose to call a friend or attend a twelve-step meeting to attend to the deeper issues. If our daily donut masks pathos or stress, we can address those challenges directly, rather than simply burying them under empty calories and a sugar glaze.

Practice:
A New Relationship with Anger

(1) Bring to mind a frustrating interpersonal event. It can be anything that you found irritating, such as a small interaction or hearing some unpleasant news. It should be something that, when you think about it, fills your mind with thoughts of how unfair or difficult life can be, or how unhelpful others can be.

(2) Instead of retelling the entire story in your mind, just hold a single image that best evokes the irritating nature of this experience. What you are doing here is actually inviting the emotion of

frustration or disappointment to arise. At the same time, keep yourself comfortable, with your arms and legs relaxed.

(3) Hold the provocative image in your mind and patiently activate your feelings of irritation, frustration, or disappointment until you can feel them stirring somewhere in the front of your body—in the belly, chest, throat, and/or face.

Try to create a welcoming environment for these feelings. Resistance only makes the anger stronger and more painful, and will stimulate the "unfairness of it all" thought that gets us nowhere. Create a space where the emotion can play out, without trying to get rid of anything.

(4) Every time your mind tries to intervene and retell the story, or launches into criticisms or ideas about the way the world should be, bring it back again to the body. If you can locate feelings of frustration or disappointment in the body, you can send soothing, nurturing messages from the mind to the feeling itself: "It's okay. You're allowed to feel that way. You're safe now." Connect with the anger the way you would talk to a child you love and who is upset. It's not the words that matter here. It's the caring voice and calming awareness with which you greet your feeling that matters.

10. NO WAY OUT BUT THROUGH

SPIRITUAL PRACTICE is not a bypass that allows us to sidestep difficult feelings. We need to be able to sit with and hold even what is difficult. It's not about being above it all; it's about being with it all.

The Spiritual Bypass

The drive to try to feel secure as often as possible, and to avoid what's uncomfortable, is universal. But there's no way to avoid aging, sickness, frustrating events, and eventual, but inevitable, separations from loved ones. If we don't develop the wisdom to discern this, we'll take measures to sidestep any and all of life's unavoidable, painful experiences. Eventually our attempts to avoid the inevitable—such as resorting to substance abuse—backfire horribly, leaving people both wounded and dependent upon the damaging behaviors.

On a less extreme level we may choose more socially acceptable though equally unskillful avoidance strategies. We manage loneliness with television viewing. We alleviate feelings of purposelessness with shopping. We manage feelings of emptiness by bingeing on food, and so forth. Of course these strategies fail to satisfy us. As we quickly habituate to them, we have to go to the well more often while feeling less and less satisfied. Ultimately we wind up more miserable and frustrated than in the beginning.

We may even turn to apparently more skillful means of stress reduction, such as yoga, exercise, playing fetch with the dog, or learning to meditate. We may seek a spiritual escape from our emotions and mistake the initial elation as a form of emotional health. I know I did! Throughout the first twenty years of my practice I hoped meditation would provide some kind of spiritual immunity from frustration, anger, envy or loneliness. When my depression first appeared, I even sought counsel from monks to see if perhaps I was meditating wrong.

I know, as a meditation teacher, that I cannot claim that practice will lead to a life without frustration, sadness, or disappointment. I can only claim that spiritual practice will help us hold our difficult emotions.

The desire to be without core emotional experiences is just another form of craving. Using spiritual endeavor to bypass emotions is just another avoidance tendency, like workaholism, rumination, or escape through books, television, or video games.

While spiritual bypasses may seem healthier than slamming back a few drinks to cope with the day's stressful disappointments, all forms of bypass have the same ultimate goal: to disconnect us from feeling and holding difficult emotions. There's nothing healthy about using spiritual practice to escape our feelings. It's a form of self-harm to tell ourselves we shouldn't feel. Many of our emotions are unpleasant, but they're necessary nonetheless. There is anger, fear, and sadness in life, whether we like it or not. Attempting to circumvent these states creates even greater suppressive tendencies.

The suttas tell us that emotions are founded on feelings (*vedanas*), which occur when objects are regarded as desirable or unpleasant. When I see a bagel lovingly smeared with cream cheese, a pleasant feeling (*sukkha vedana*) emphasizes the bagel's desirability, compelling me toward it; if I stumble upon the bagel months later, now rotten with mold and decay, a felt sense of disgust (*dukkha vedana*) impels me to move away from it as a repellant object. Often such feelings are subtle or unconscious, but I am still moved by them.

Throughout the course of each day I seldom have enough time or information to properly deliberate on every decision I make, and so relying on reasoning alone would be impractical. Instead, when I make a wise choice in life, it is often because I have noted and followed an underlying physical impulse. When I make an effort to skip the junk food and eat a healthy, light meal with leafy green vegetables, my body feels good in the long term, which, over time, rewards me and encourages me to buy more in the future.

There are also times when gut feelings and intuition can steer us in the wrong direction. Perhaps in my early years, a grade school teacher wearing a brown cardigan shames me before a classroom of giggling students: I may well grow up to feel suspicious of everyone wearing a brown cardigan. Perhaps if I get food poisoning from one food or another, I'll feel repulsed by it, forever after, even if I know it has been handled properly. Our unconscious behaviors are largely driven by associations, and associations can be misleading. Given that human beings are social animals and need interaction to help us regulate our emotions and to bounce our gut ideas off each other, it's invariably a good idea to share our impulses with a wise friend for counsel.

The Buddha didn't seem to find much, if any, value in what gut feelings convey. In sutta after sutta feelings are referred to as *baits of the world, impermanent, defiled, that which should be overcome on the way to reason.* In the *Nibbedhika Sutta* the Buddha defines the eightfold path as "the way leading to the ending of feeling." In the *Vedana Sutta* the Buddha asserts that any feelings are defilements, states of awareness to be abandoned if the mind is inclined to release and liberation. The path to liberation is taught to lead from disenchantment with clinging and craving to a state of tranquil dispassion, or *viraga*, and then to true freedom.

It's important not to downplay the contrast between our current psychological insights and the early Buddhist Dharma on this issue. This may be why some practitioners arrive at my classes hoping that they'll be able to learn how to sidestep all the difficult feelings that arise throughout the course of day. But hoping to live without anxiety or anger is like wanting to paint without ever using dark colors on our canvas. I'm not surprised people so deeply believe there's a spiritual bypass, searching for a way to meditate that will spare them feeling lonely, as many Buddhist teachers present themselves in a honeyed demeanor that suggests they have transcended anxious thoughts.

Negative emotions—such as anger or sadness—are often vital messengers conveying important truths: we're unhappy in our jobs, unfulfilled in our relationships, sensing something is amiss in our friendships. Putting aside feelings is no more preferable than ignoring the sounds of a smoke alarm in a burning building. Worse than that: repressing the awareness of feelings via distractions or soothing substances invariably leads to future calamities. During the years I repressed my social anxieties with alcohol, I wound up following far more detrimental impulses, which led me to further self-sabotaging behaviors, including poor romantic choices and reckless spending habits.

My Friend Jake

One of my closest friends, Jake, was sober for three memorable years. I met him in the first six months of his recovery from a heroin addiction that, when he was hitting bottom, found him robbing coke dealers to pay for ten bags a day. On one occasion his getaway car was shot full of holes, which somehow didn't deter him from attempting to rob the same dealer on a subsequent occasion. At the beginning of our friendship, Jake was on a methadone maintenance program, working as pedicab driver, pedaling tourists around midtown Manhattan eight hours a day. Over the course of two years, he incrementally lowered his methadone dose. At times it was an agonizing process to watch: chills, nausea, bone-aching pain. I can't imagine what it was like for him to live through.

He managed to spend a year completely clean. He started a band, acted in a wonderful short art film, and made many friends with his mischievous sense of humor. But his time in the sun was far too short. On a late October afternoon, riding home from his carpentry job, he was hit by a car. Thrown from his bike, his leg was broken in multiple spots. Jake wound up undergoing a serious operation to repair the leg, but the pain required opiates to manage, and before long heroin was back in the picture. Our last few meetings during that final month are deeply etched in my mind: memories as haunting and painful as they get. On a cold February evening a phone call from a mutual friend brought the news we feared, though somehow still didn't consider possible. Jake was found by his landlord, sitting upright in his living room, a needle still in his arm, surrounded by spent bags of dope, lifeless.

Feeling Grief

We shouldn't try to soothe or minimize grief at death. Emotional pain isn't healed by reason. Healing begins with acceptance and connecting with others—empathy. We all have to lose someone eventually.

For life to have any meaning, we must be open to and feel death, offering it all the grief and despair it deserves. I find nothing less healing or meaningful than the platitudes many people offer when they discover someone has lost a loved one. When my parents died, a year apart, I politely cut people off before they could finish platitudes such as "Well, your father lived a long life," or "Your mother is at peace." While their intentions were good, there is a far less skillful agenda lurking: As a culture, we shun and turn away from death, as it highlights the futility of our own endeavors. We don't like to see others mourn, as their loss reminds us of the precariousness of our own relationships. But the experience of death should not be relieved, or reduced.

Distracting the grieving from their painful feelings may seem to be a form of care, but I see it as a form of harm. Even if we can distract another's torment for a brief respite, it only postpones and exacerbates the pain that will, sooner or later, surge into awareness.

Trying to minimize grief is like running from one's shadow; the times in our lives when we truly suffer are when we don't stop to feel our emotions. Yes, during such times we may think about the loss, play and replay the stories, but that is not the same as feeling the hollowness, despair, and confusion.

How to Make Any Sense Out of It

It's commonplace for people to believe that what makes the human mind so special and powerful is that it has provided us with language and logic—and these are, of course, very powerful tools. We can create and retell the stories of our days. We can transform stumbling blocks into life lessons. We can learn to discern harmless from harmful impulses.

Our inner chatter will accompany us throughout our most frightening and overwhelming experiences, creating a sense of inner companionship.

Its not surprising that after life's most painful emotional events we listen avidly to this inner voice as it tries to make sense of it all, fully convinced it can uncover meaning and transcribe experience into ideas we can conveniently carry around and remind ourselves when necessary.

We cherish the conceptual, representational, narrative mind, so it's no surprise that our stories are sustained by neural circuits largely associated with the brain's left hemisphere, which is the dominant hemisphere of adult life. The left hemisphere of the brain is by nature optimistic and advantage seeking, believing that any problem, any situation in life can be abstracted, turned into a rule, and solved. If we can just find enough time to think, and the right way to encapsulate a painful tangle of events, then a hidden meaning will emerge, and with it safety, inoculation from pain. After relationship separations, career reversals, and financial setbacks, the narrating mind spins out its stories, providing a sense of security: this won't happen again, if I can only figure out what went wrong. And so much of mental life is a ceaseless quest for the perfect, transcendent understanding of life, a pursuit which has no doubt dogged humankind since the dawn of our species.

All of this leaves out the fact that *the brain has two hemispheres, not one.* And the right hemisphere, which so often works diligently in the background producing our emotional and attentional impulses, focuses on other concerns entirely.

NO WAY OUT BUT THROUGH

A dominant agenda of these circuits is guiding us to connect securely with other people and situations. We are, after all, social animals, and connection is our bread and butter, the key to our species survival. Our needs to connect are expressed essentially via emotions—we experience joy when we feel socially accepted, and pain after rejections.

While our emotional circuits don't have the abundant language abilities of the left hemisphere, it continually communicates to us through the physical body. When disappointing events occur, our obsessive thoughts distract us from an array of emotional messages: contraction of the brow, tightness in the jaw and throat, a sense of hollowness in the chest, and tight abdominal muscles. The emotional mind continually signals us when our priorities have skewed toward achieving rewards over sustaining meaningful relationships by creating negative emotional states. If we go through a breakup, emotional circuits create sadness, grief. If we do something that harms others, guilt arises (if we are not sociopathic).

Quite often we don't appreciate the truths of our emotional pain. Our cognitive apparatus helps us evade the loneliness, grief, sorrow by producing alluring smokescreens, obsessive thoughts, and ongoing inner chatter that keeps us distracted with resentments and self-righteous indignation: "How dare they? Why did they do that? Why did I do this? What should have been done different?" In other words, our inner verbiage is the place where we seek refuge from the inevitable wounds of life.

The stories we tell ourselves—how life should have been different, how this or that shouldn't have happened—might very well be true, but how much do they really solve? The longer we're enraptured by these narratives, the worse the underlying wounds become. They don't just go away because we ignore them. Eventually the wounds pile up and erupt in anxiety attacks, rage, addiction, binges—the tantrums of the ignored inner child.

When we don't listen to our bodies, feelings, and moods, we rely on addictive strategies to push our nonverbal experiences out of awareness. We might shop. I have an abnormal collection of hoodies, more than I'll ever need. When I was working at the advertising job I loathed, I fell into the habit of rewarding myself for working yet another week by purchasing CDs. I wound up with an absurdly large collection of music I no longer listen to or care about.

The rising of abandoned emotions creates insomnia. We suddenly become frantically busy, incapable of settling down, for to stop, pause, relax would draw our attention to sensations we're desperately trying to avoid. Eventually we'll fall into avoidance strategies: the repressed, vulnerable, wounded child starts to signal itself through the cracks in our voices, the sadness in our eyes.

Representational thought has the additional tendency of reducing and simplifying our experiences into the same old story—*others are against me, I'm invariably being misunderstood, I'm entirely innocent or doing the best I can while others are often nefarious, mean-spirited, naive, etc.* Thus we're able to excuse ourselves from investigating each moment from more challenging perspectives that might be more informative.

My work with practitioners has demonstrated that skillfully understanding painful events asks that we put aside our tendencies to try and "figure it out." To uncover any understanding of life demands far greater investigation and vulnerability than most of us anticipate. That which makes sense of life's powerful experiences cannot be conveyed in language-based thought alone; deep understandings of loss cannot be captured in trite sayings. The rush to try to alleviate loss with "Well, at least he lived a long life and got to see Paris before the cancer spread . . ." shows how desperate we are not to feel negative emotions, which in turn leads us toward tilted and incorrect interpretations.

I'd like to propose that there are three types of right understanding that must be present for our comprehension of an experience to be accurate, insightful, and of any spiritual value.

The first is that *meaning occurs across multiple levels*; it's not found only in a process of thinking. Meaning is something that is felt: that is experienced in the body, is expressed in our behaviors, is present in the way we breathe, is seen in the way we carry ourselves. It's physiological as much as it is psychological. The need to always try to translate an experience into an idea or speech inherently does violence to the complexities of life's events. Our lived human quality is not just a bunch of words floating through the mind. Experience contains physiological feelings of heaviness, jumpy attention, tears, sadness, states of not knowing. And these are just as meaningful as thought. In fact, in many ways, they're often more meaningful than the inner speeches we feel the need to add on.

The Buddha's profound teaching that mindfulness should begin with the body and then move to the emotions, as we discussed in chapter 6, was echoed by William James, who proposed that emotions and physiological sensations arise before thought. Our emotional signals are far more complex and nuanced than thought, which always tries to simplify experience into predictable narrative. If we wish to make sense of our lives, to carve out understanding after the break up or a loss, we're on the right track if we forgo trying to "figure it out," and choose instead to simply observe whatever arises.

This brings me to the second proposal, which is that *meaning takes a lot of time*. It's never something that happens quickly. Full integration of the felt means that we cannot rush toward any form of "making sense." Instead, we must turn toward our pain. I know after my friend Lauren died, killed on her bike by a careless driver, I felt a strong impulse to try to make sense of it all rather than attend to the feelings of loss and sadness and emptiness. My thoughts tried desperately to turn it into some kind of story, to really make sense of the unfathomable, but I fought against the impulse, reflecting in my practice that true understanding of such a tragedy takes a very long time. It's similar to how, after a devastating, painful breakup, we rush to simplistic conclusions such as "Well, that will teach me what happens if you date a Canadian." We gravitate toward pronouncements, invariably in the hope of numbing what needs to be felt in the stomach, heart, throat, face, breath. It's only years later when a deeper truth appears: "What was I thinking? That person was on a totally different path from me. They wanted something completely different from life; we were never that compatible!" To arrive at a place where we can be with and process an array of emotions, which is necessary before any right understanding is possible, requires allowing anger and sadness and frustration to appear, be held, and gradually diminish. Not attending to grief or pain leads toward a hollow interpretation of our connections and losses.

So before we reach the last proposition, let's review: (1) Meaning cannot be fully expressed in thought, but requires feelings and emotion; (2) Meaning doesn't appear quickly but invariably takes time. My third proposition is that *understanding always requires intimate interaction with others*, that true insight, an accurate appraisal of experience, can rarely if ever be developed in isolation, on our own. As the human mind tends to avoid the uncomfortable, and leans to repress difficult emotions, unearthing a true appreciation of important events demands interaction and mutual support. When we express our experience through nonverbal expressions and gestures, and when our trembling voice articulates our pain to another human being, then we can find a right-sized response and allow our simplistic thoughts to be gently elevated.

In contrast to the privileged status afforded to verbal cognition, interpersonal connection, I believe, lies at the core of all healing. In my experience the more a practitioner facilitates the emotional experience and expression of others, the more they in turn evidence positive changes in their lives.

What this means is that when I talk to you about my

EMOTIONAL REASONING: UNDERSTANDING YOURSELF

sadness, my loss, my dismay, I don't convey it in words alone. But somehow when I explain it or talk to you, the cracks in my voice, the emotions in my face, my body language, the hesitation in my voice lets you see the emotion creeping through. Then I will look at your emotional expressions and I will begin to align with them. Human beings implicitly co-regulate; while we talk and exchange ideas, unconsciously we gravitate to the same emotional tone as each other. This helps us make sense of experience in a way that we never can alone.

Holding Emotions

Practice:
RAIN

Tara Brach and Michele McDonald developed a practice called RAIN that emphasizes mindfulness as non-judgmental. Over my years of teaching this practice, I've modified it somewhat to the following four steps:

- *Recognize* what is going on;

- *Allow* the experience to be there, just as it is;

- *Investigate* with kindness;

- *Nurture*, which asks that we relate to our internal experience with care and compassion, rather than resistance or frustration.

Allowing thoughts, emotions, or bodily sensations to arise doesn't mean agreeing or disagreeing with them; instead, we simply acknowledge the presence of such energies, be they comfortable or unpleasant. The process asks that we feel what is present, weighing our feelings and impulses against the input of reason. In this way it helps us to consider both our rational thoughts and our emotional feelings.

While every tool in the Dharma has its uses, when they're hijacked by our avoidance strategies and defense mechanisms, they'll lead to only more suffering in life. While there are many helpful benefits of sustained spiritual practice—such as better self-regulation, improved mood and health—it cannot reprogram the emotional processes that are meant to be felt, attended to, and processed.

Thankfully liberation is not a state without emotions, even the difficult ones, such as despair, fear, disgust, anger. (Without feeling anger we cannot confront social injustice or establish secure boundaries; without sadness we cannot process loss; without fear . . . well, you get it.) From my time spent attending to great nuns and monks during retreats, I believe that liberation consists of greater equanimity and emotional balance. It is a state in which emotions and sensations can be held and tolerated without adding additional reactivity or suffering, but there are still difficult emotions to be experienced. So spiritual growth should not be seen as the achievement of lasting elation. To be a spiritual practitioner entails being available and open to whatever is present, no matter what the sensations and energies are, without letting anything define us.

Practice:
Noting Emotions in a Safe Container

Set an intention to put aside, if only for a little while, thoughts that concern events that are not actually occurring right here and now. When such thoughts arise just note them, and remind yourself you can return to them later. Don't push them away. Simply allow them to remain in the background.

Take three deep, full breaths, tensing the body on the inhalations, relaxing during long, smooth exhalations. Think to yourself "May I find true, lasting peace within" to help relax the mind and override unresolved life dramas we're carrying around in our thoughts. This practice should be heartily developed by those who have trouble letting go of the word-based, chatty narrator of the mind.

Locate and focus awareness on body sensations that occur with each in-and-out breath. Don't visualize how you look, just feel the inner sensations. Follow these sensations by noting how they move through the body, such as the sensation flowing up from the abdomen to the chest with in-breaths and back down with out-breaths.

Locate a *resting place* in the body where the mind can return during the pauses between breaths. The belly is an excellent possibility. Staying present during these pauses requires the greatest effort.

After a while release the focus on the breath, and open the mind to anything that seeks your attention, including the thoughts you put aside during the first step of this practice.

As each thought, image, or external sensation arises in the mind, notice the accompanying sensations that arise in the body.

Identify or label these feelings as emotions. For example muscle contractions in the abdomen during a worrisome daydream might be labeled "fear," while a feeling of tightness in the chest arising during an unpleasant memory might feel like disappointment.

Accept these feelings without resistance or judgment; don't try to change or push away the experience. If the sensations are overwhelming, relax other areas of the body and extend the exhalations.

Stay detached from the thoughts and stories that try to pull you away from the somatic experience. Keep the mind in a state where it doesn't identify with anything, but rather notes and observes.

After observing the emotional state for a while, bring to mind a reassuring phrase of self-love and kindness, such as "I care about you, I'll take care of you." Remember all feelings convey messages they believe are in our best interests; while they can be misguided, they are like children that need our attention and care.

11. GREETING WHAT HIDES IN THE SHADOWS

Why Being Genuine Is So Difficult

WE SURVIVE BY connecting to others. That's our advantage. We can bond, share information, act as a team.

We are born into an extremely vulnerable state as infants. We need other people to help us survive. If we are abandoned, we will suffer, if not die. Our natural expression of emotion—wailing in fear, kicking in frustration, purging something that disgusts, giggling when happy—are messages sent to our caretakers expressing our needs and feelings. If our caretakers understand and respond, we'll be comfortable expressing them in the future. If, for some reason, our emotions are poorly tolerated, we may learn to suppress them. The need to belong and survive is far stronger than the need to express our spontaneous, natural feelings.

Many of us start out life with many spontaneous, true impulses—singing aloud, hopping, crying, hiding, making food art on tablecloths and crayon paintings on walls. We begin entirely unaware of social norms. Then, in a million interactions with our caretakers, teachers, and peers, we experience abandonment, shame, rejection, and scorn until we conform (by thinking and feeling as we were told) or comply (by acting as if we thought and felt that way). So we learn to suppress our anger and discontent. Every time we felt an emotional impulse that threatened core relationships, we automatically flipped a switch and changed to a behavior that restored connection. As children we sacrifice much to maintain attachment.

We've constructed a false self, a set of inauthentic behaviors performed to win acceptance at all costs—for infants and children, feeling disconnected from a caretaker feels akin to annihilation, so we'll suppress our most authentic feelings to maintain a secure base with our caretakers. We may not have been interested in basketball or hockey in the slightest, but we watched and cheered enough to be accepted. We bend and twist and desperately conform in any manner of ways in the hopes that others will like us. Any emotions, memories, and impulses that result in interpersonal rejection are not only inconvenient, but painful. If others pull away from us when we tell them about our sadness, we suffer and learn to conceal it. There's nothing more frightening than being excluded from the pack.

So we have all learned to pack away difficult emotions and complicated memories associated with abandonment or disconnection. We've stuffed them into our shadow selves. However, the emotional content we keep hidden from ourselves and others doesn't go away; it becomes thoroughly disproportionate and impossible to regulate. The repressed stays fearful and vulnerable—it is unaware that we can withstand pain in life.

Creation of the Shadow Realm

These unwanted impulses—fear, anger, weakness, confusion, doubt—continue to express themselves in situations in which we feel threatened and vulnerable, as they're deeply attached to survival impulses. We can remove these impulses and memories from the conscious realm, but they'll remain fully intact, waiting to come back out.

The shadow self sees threats where there are none. The shadow self has been kept away from conscious experience and daily life, unaware of our current strengths and capabilities; now that we're adults, we're less vulnerable, and we're capable of handling many of the threats we couldn't survive as a child. But our fear, which has so often been suppressed, isn't aware of our current skills, so it can trigger anxiety in perfectly harmless situations.

Many of us are have parents who were divorced. When a parent leaves, the experience is naturally traumatic. The upheaval will be deeply threatening. The memories and emotions will often wind up repressed as shadow content. If these feelings and memories remain continually buried, without being given any attention, the abandoned child grows into an adult who cannot process the inevitable interpersonal rejections and losses of adult life. They'll experience someone breaking off a two-month-long relationship with the same force and upheaval as a child abandoned by a parent. They'll ruminate, experience insomnia, stalk their ex's Facebook page, send a flurry of escalating text messages, cry endlessly. The emotional content we keep hidden from ourselves and others doesn't go away; it becomes thoroughly disproportionate and impossible to regulate. The repressed stays fearful and vulnerable; it is unaware that we can withstand pain in life. When breakups occur, the adult child will fall apart, regress to clinging or protest behavior, attach to extreme thoughts: "I'll never find anyone else."

When we repress perfectly human, natural inclinations— such as fear, or impulses that don't fit gender expectations— into the shadow realm, what are left in their place are feelings of emptiness. Instead of feeling the locked jaw, furrowed forehead, tight chest, and shaking rage that arises with anger, we feel nothing. *Suppression leads to a hollowing out.* We are not born with feelings of emptiness. The origination of feelings of lack and depletion is the all-too-inevitable result of repression; we'll feel, in moods and the body, what has been condemned to our shadow self, but it remains outside of conscious awareness.

Worse than this, when we don't express our hidden inclinations, they'll remain entirely unregulated. The emotions that we haven't learned to express with others will cause anxiety, even panic.

How to Handle the Shadow

When we continually repress difficult energies and emotions, failing to create a safe container that allows them to arise for attention, they don't go away quietly. They'll slip out and cause conflict with others. If we don't learn to calmly express frustrations to our spouses, we'll find ourselves getting into petty arguments and debates with them in the future.

Even those impulses that are truly harmful and should in no way be acted out in reality—for example, rage at some relative's political views—still must be provided with attention; we must acknowledge the tension in our shoulders and note the violent imagery of our thoughts, or we'll find ourselves acting poorly in the future. Maybe we will write a snide or inflammatory post on Facebook down the line, for instance.

Our repressive tendencies lead to sad, unwanted ends: If we're incapable of expressing sadness, if we can only allow others to see our funny or intellectual sides, we'll never truly, intimately connect with other people. We'll never know true love and acceptance. We'll live a plastic life.

The shadow self should not be an inconvenient passenger in life. When attended to skillfully, it's what allows us to achieve true intimate connections with others. For it's only when we express, through words, gestures, and body language, the entire palette of our human experience, both the uncomplicated and the embarrassing, that we can be truly loved. When we conceal our discomfort and shameful experiences, we are not open and cannot feel accepted by others. It's only when we risk showing others the entirety of our emotional experience that we know true love.

Even the Buddha had a shadow self, a "dark passenger" referred to in the canon as Mara. Mara is the return of the

Buddha's repressed carnal impulses, all that he has jettisoned along his six-year spiritual journey: his addictions to sensual pleasures, power, anger, fear, boredom, anxiety, inclinations that hinder calm, peaceful abiding. There is a tendency to think of Mara as a wholly external demon, but in the suttas, he reminds the Buddha that he cannot be escaped, because he arises wherever thoughts arise. In the *Padhana Sutta*, the Buddha echoes:

> Buddha: "Mara, your domain is our sight, hearing, taste, smell, touch, thoughts, and ideas. Where consciousness depends on these features, you will exist; where consciousness doesn't depend on these factors, you will not exist."
> Mara: "If your thoughts and ideas are here then you can't escape from me."
> Buddha: "What they speak of—thoughts and ideas—aren't mine, we do not claim them, therefore you won't be able to find me."

The Buddha also said,

> Mara, your forces are not of the world and cannot be defeated externally; only our insight can constrain your force.

The Buddha calmly addressed his shadow self with the words, "I see you, Mara." He doesn't scold or chase Mara away. When Mara scorns the Buddha, doubting his enlightenment, demanding a witness, the Buddha touches the ground with his hand, and the Earth itself announces: "I am the witness." Again he does not speak directly against Mara. And as the first glimmer of morning appears in the sky, just by this calm acknowledgment, Mara has been attended to and voluntarily recedes from view.

This story presents us with a path toward emotional growth and healing: it tells us to encounter all that has been consigned to the shadows, to feel and hear our doubts, frustrations, and fears, to calmly acknowledge these feelings.

Practice:
Welcome Mara!

Notice when an issue or topic activates what the Buddha called *papanca*, or obsessive, repetitive thinking. For example, I often find thoughts of financial insecurity—"Will I have enough money to survive if I grow old?"—to be quite insistent, not to mention dismaying, as they can paint some pretty vivid pictures of how bad the future could get for me. I find that trying to distract myself from financial insecurity rarely succeeds for long; perhaps I'm a naturally gifted worrier, but the thoughts of homelessness and poverty can spring back if I resist them.

In Mara practice, however, I simply greet the arising of insecurity with "Welcome, Mara!" I no longer view my insecurity as a nuisance, something that needs to be defeated, argued away, dismissed, conquered. There's no agenda to get rid of anything; the goal becomes to "be with" the thoughts. Ironically, when we welcome even the most persistent, unwanted thought, we'll find that the thought starts to return less frequently and carries less of punch. After greeting the thought, provide an assurance that it's allowed to stay in the mind, don't give it your undivided attention; continue focusing on whatever task is at hand. So my financial security can start to project its horror movies in the mind, and I won't fight it. I'll continue to remove the resistance and give it permission, while focusing on whatever else requires my attention.

When accepted into awareness, even the most unrelenting fears or resentments can be accommodated; like in the Buddhist legend of Milarepa, when we allow the demons to stay in our cave, they begin to lose their strength. It seems that nothing gives obsessive thoughts more force and intimidation than resistance.

12. THE ROAD THAT WE ARE MOST AFRAID TO TAKE OFTEN LEADS TO LIBERATION

IF WE'RE ABLE to identify the many tactics and habitual behaviors we use to keep our shadow self concealed from view, we can make headway against the process of repression. After long-term Buddhist therapy and many years of providing one-on-one mentoring to hundreds of people, I've encountered a wide array of strategies and tactics used to avoid facing what's difficult about ourselves.

Many people will recognize these as "defense mechanisms," while others will think of them as Buddhist "hindrances." Both are equally valid descriptions; they're all forms of self-delusion. What follows is a brief summary of some of the most common forms of inhibition.

Busyness

I keep myself busy, scheduled, racing from one obligation to the next. Overscheduling helps me stay a few steps ahead of my feelings of frustration and grief. Busyness may seem to be the hallmark of "getting things done," but it's actually motivated by fear: if I'm hustling and overloaded, I won't have to feel lost, I won't have to ask myself if my life is purposeful, my relationships meaningful. I won't stop and attend to body sensations, through which my shadow self professes its urges and inclinations. A tight chest reveals how unconnected I've become, a contracted abdomen how vulnerable I feel, a lack of energy and sparkle conveys how little purpose and meaning I'm feeling in life. To be invariably busy is to be disconnected from truth, which announces itself in the quiet moments when I stop and become aware of what's aching to be felt beneath the parade of external sensations.

Projection

The mind can be like a projector, casting unwanted emotions and impulses onto others as if they're movie screens. Often we're not actually seeing or hearing what's actually occurring, just our own "stuff." Anger is not an emotional state I handle easily, so when I'm furious with someone, I can project the feeling onto them, seeing their actions as aggressive and hostile—then I'll judge them for being ill-tempered.

Interestingly, many practitioners I've worked with in mentoring seem to gravitate toward romantic partners based on projection; if they've repressed their impulsive, spontaneous urges, preferring to take very deliberate steps in life, they'll be attracted to individuals who act more instinctively; those who seek to stay surrounded by large groups of friends, who prefer to build consensus and coalitions, are often drawn to isolating, contrary, antisocial individualists.

Excessive Sleep

Most of us have used sleep as a form of avoidance now and then. Sleep and grogginess are the inverse of busyness, but both are avoidance strategies that keep difficult emotional experiences out of touch. Very often, when I'm most tired when sitting still, if I really pay attention, I'll locate an emotional activation that is aching to be felt, right beneath the surface of awareness.

Compartmentalization

If we keep feelings and impulses repressed, out of sight, like an animal locked in a closet, given any opening or opportunity, it will express itself frantically.

Years ago I worked with someone who grew up in a family where sexual behavior was shamed and certainly not discussed openly. Sexual impulses felt particularly threatening: his parents expressed little physical tenderness; his mother condemned even the most innocent displays of sexual behavior on television. So as an adult, he experienced discomfort over his sensual impulses. And so he would ritualistically act out his sexual urges by skulking into a sex shop to find release by masturbating in a video booth. This ritual was thoroughly compartmentalized from the rest of his life and a significant source of shame, to the degree it was acknowledged at all; while sexuality is a completely natural impulse, it had become so demonized and shamed that the only way it could be expressed was as a hidden, joyless routine.

I've also counseled people who have struggled with eating disorders, such as binging and purging. In many cases I've heard a similar pattern of individuals growing up in controlling, intrusive environments where their caretakers provided little freedom or emotional tolerance. Under such strict surveillance, even having an appetite created a sense of unease, bringing unwanted attention and a lifetime proclivity toward acting out urges in secret, followed by denial.

Idealizing

Many people I work with have tendencies to project onto others entirely unrealistic, exaggerated qualities. Idealizing is quite common in the beginning of relationships. Many of us have strong tendencies to aggrandize the qualities of a new lover. "He's perfect. This is the one. Everything is so great. We never argue. We agree on everything." Contemporary neuroscience offers some fascinating insights into the process of idealization and why it's so common. Suppose a friend becomes infatuated with someone they regularly encounter at their gym. When passing their crush, perhaps at the running machines, they may feel a tingling jolt of energy up the spine, even a surge of elation. These are the telltale neural boosts of dopamine—which also produce the rewards for purchasing an item at an astonishingly reduced price. Given how pleasant these reward states are, it's no wonder our brains can so easily become obsessed with individuals; we're unconsciously reactivating feel-good chemicals, just as an addict returns to a favorite intoxicant. And there's more than dopamine involved: excitatory adrenal chemicals are activated, providing a sense of thrill and drama, not to mention obsession. These charged reward states tend to override the brain's alarm system, which is why it's so easy to only see the positive attributes of a new romantic partner or friend, to become infatuated with the wrong person. In such states many of us have lapses in judgment—rushing into sex, cohabitation, loaning or investing money, etc.

During the early stages of a relationship, the states of euphoria and drama tend to result in a systemic repression of negative emotions; we overlook the discouraging exchanges and disappointing remarks. Later on, however, as the encounters activate less dopamine and adrenaline, all the repressed resentments, which have been mounting up and stored unconsciously, burst through into consciousness . . . we'll no longer see any of their positive qualities, only the negatives. At which point the other person is seen in an entirely different light: he or she is selfish, narcissistic, sociopathic, etc.—how could we not see it before?

As a Dharma teacher, I find that many people have a tendency to project onto me entirely unrealistic, exaggerated qualities. People have told me, without irony or sarcasm, "Well, of course *you* never get bored/frustrated/angry/etc." It's hard not to laugh, but I keep a straight face; it's my job to be empathetic. And quite often, when I hear this from a practitioner, it means they're struggling to accept their own frustration, or whatever emotion they're claiming I've magically risen above. This results in a consciousness that is poorly integrated and that resists entirely human moods.

Many I've worked with will also claim, when we first sit down to talk, that their childhoods were perfect: "I had wonderful parents." Two months later the story invariably changes, as one story after the next of unmet needs and lack of emotional mirroring are recounted. This is not to imply that everyone's parents were dreadful, or that everyone I meet with was emotionally abused. But the times we don't have our needs met in childhood can feel so annihilating, so deeply threatening, that it's difficult to feel the rejection, even decades later, much less acknowledge what happened. So, rather than having a realistic account of their lives, many live in fantasies.

In my own therapy with a terrific Buddhist therapist, I slowly realized that my mother was not the saint I had claimed, that there were many times I felt she used work as an escape from my alcoholic father, abandoning me to the care of a monster. Such a realization didn't mean she was any less lovable. In fact, realizing my disappointments allowed my love for her to become actual, rather than saccharine and delusional.

Rationalizing

This happens when one explains away their emotion-based behavior as if it were an entirely rational decision. I've struggled with this penchant for most of my life and probably always will. In my first years of therapy and Buddhist teacher training, others noted it, quite frequently. Years ago I sat for a while with a Buddhist teacher whom I later learned had cheated on his wife with a student. After this revelation I eviscerated his views and insights. Others pointed out that my criticism was concealing my anger and disappointment at his behavior.

Rationalization is common when we don't feel comfortable acknowledging the emotions guiding our choices. I once heard a friend say, when questioned about impulsively asking a new girlfriend to cohabitate, "Yes, of course, I asked her to move in. This way we won't have to pay as much rent." He was too embarrassed to acknowledge that his loneliness and need for companionship played any role in the decision.

Preoccupation

Preoccupation is the tendency to fixate on a single relationship, often a romance, so I can avoid all of my mounting feelings of depression lingering in the background: my sense of hollowness or lack of real purpose, my lack of serenity, the paucity of creativity in the rest of my life. If I've allowed my life to become an empty routine of worry and work, or simply worry, fixating on someone who isn't returning my calls feels safer: I don't have to focus on what really needs attention. What I really need isn't one person to make life okay, I need a wide range of meaningful human connections if I am to live a rich, purposeful, meaningful life.

But There's No Need to Feel Overwhelmed

In this chapter I've addressed some of the psychological challenges I regularly encounter while working with practitioners.

Yet despite the depth and tenacity of our emotional struggles, in the course of a series of honest and empathetic encounters between myself and the other person, substantial healing of deep emotional wounds can not only be expected, but will often occur over a relatively brief period of time.

As we humans are pack animals, we can experience so much pain as a result of damaged relationships and exclusions, but the inverse is true as well: once we find a tolerant and patient individual who can hear and hold our suffering with us, the revival of the heart can be astonishing. Once we really feel seen by another, held in their sympathetic gaze, there is no grief that cannot be soothed. The following chapters delve deeper into how healing occurs in relationships and Buddhist mentoring.

13. PUTTING IT ALL ON THE LINE

IN ORDER TO authentically and securely connect with other human beings, first we must dare to connect with what has been consigned to the shadows. Without opening to it, without being able to hold it, we'll never know a true, deep bond, and that's a truly dark outcome.

Unfortunately those impulses and memories that have been covered up for decades do not appear in smooth, personable guises. Because we rarely share them with others, we haven't learned to regulate them. The solution is to share them with other people carefully.

It's only when we learn to talk to others about our anger, for instance, that we can express it honestly, without repressing it until it bursts out in rage. It's only when we can communicate our anger to others that we learn to regulate it in a way that provides attention and care, while maintaining sympathetic and empathetic connection with others. When we withhold our anger, we don't develop the ability to temper it during our interactions. When repressed frustration makes its way past all the defense mechanisms, it will burst out as completely unregulated rage. We'll shout, yell, create a scene. But when we learn to create a safe container to feel our anger, through mindfulness meditation, and then disclose it through dialogue with a wise practitioner, we can really own our experience. This is the passage to an unimpaired emotional life.

Full Disclosure

The following is a partial inventory of some of my concealed memories and impulses. Of course the identity story I've constructed for myself in the world—Dharma teacher, calm spiritual fellow, smart guy—would prefer to keep these items stowed away, rather than express them openly. I've been taught by many previous experiences that genuine, truthful disclosures can lead to abandonment, but I'll risk it once again—after all, you've read this far.

- At forty I had a complete nervous breakdown and thankfully took antidepressants to recover.

- Although I'm a Buddhist teacher, there are many times I hate to meditate, and I don't particularly enjoy long silent retreats.

- I can be very material at times; I crave new gadgets that I know will not provide any lasting happiness, yet I long for them nonetheless.

- There are times I'm envious of other people's successes, even other spiritual teachers I know well and like.

- Despite being a practitioner of thirty years, I feel times of great loneliness, confusion, doubt, sadness.

- When I was a teenager I wasn't physically attracted to anyone, though I pretended to be.

- There have been many times I've been terrible in bed, impotent, or selfish.

The world will not reward me with material dividends and sensual pleasures for revealing any of the above. I'm more likely to receive approval and acceptance by keeping my chin up and pasting on a hollow everything-is-swell smile, living utterly without the integrity of honesty and openness. Uncovering and revealing to others what has been concealed is rarely a popular endeavor; I may lose a few shallow friendships in the process.

I'm a secular Buddhist, in that I teach Buddhist insights from a perspective free of metaphysical trappings. I'm agnostic about rebirth and thoroughly uninterested in the canon's mentions of mystical attainments, such as spiritual practice rewarding us with the power to hear great distances or move through mountains, etc. There are plenty of other wonderful, wonderful teachers who do teach Buddhism as a religion or discuss rebirth in regard to karma.

What I do believe is that without spiritual practice I suffer needlessly in life; I'll fall back upon deploying the inhibitory strategies of concealment and repression, tactics that may have sufficed in my youth, when I was frightened and vulnerable, but that are self-sabotaging in the adult world.

- If you irritate me, I'll be tempted to avoid you in the future, rather than express my feelings to you in a beneficial way.

- I can default to exaggeration to keep your attention and/or amaze you while I recount my adventures in life.

- I will occasionally allow small disappointments and frustrations to build up and then express their energies through pointed jokes and ridicule.

- I will at times revert to social media as a way to mask feelings of loneliness.

I also have coping strategies that keep me entirely unaware of my natural, spontaneous feelings, which I could use to deeply connect with others. My defense mechanisms keep me from being aware of truly destructive impulses. They are not in my best interest:

- I am a recovering addict (twenty years sober) who spent nineteen years regulating my fears and frustrations via drinking alone.

- I can deny or minimize my true emotional states, answering, "How are you?" with "I'm fine," even though that's far from the case.

- I can project uncomfortable truths about myself onto other people: for example I can be ill-tempered with my wife for clinging to her views, when I can certainly be very rigid with my own.

- I can change emotional states that weren't particularly well tolerated in my family—such as disappointment with a friend's behavior—into emotional states that feel safer, such as cold, intellectual pessimism about human beings in general.

There is no arena of life where I am more likely to conceal certain emotions then the early stages of a romantic relationship. It's not easy for me to believe I will be loved for who I am. I am tempted to cover up genuine sensations of fear, doubt, or distrust, using a fraudulent mask, presenting to a potential partner unshakable confidence, syrupy sentimentality, or hellacious yoga-teacher-like "everything is beautiful may the light of love illuminate your path" pablum.

When I mentor practitioners, I use a wide variety of techniques to encourage people to reveal emotions and memories they've concealed, kept repressed. It's a process, for the repressed invariably creates signal anxiety when it starts to surface. Often people have kept memories, emotions, and sexual impulses out of awareness for so long that they can no longer distinguish clearly what is genuine, spontaneous, and natural from what is essentially a false behavior developed through the course of life to win a little acceptance and attention. It's sad to note, but I've seen it all too often, that true needs can be suppressed or inhibited for so long that they become extremely difficult, or even impossible, to recover.

Like most people, I have a secret reservoir of painful emotions and memories that my rational mind will go to great lengths to keep hidden, out of view. When emotions I've repressed threaten to break through into conscious awareness, at the very least I'll feel a good deal of anxiety.

When a particularly unpleasant memory, hidden in the shadows of the mind for decades, starts to arise, havoc is often the result. I've met with practitioners who, just before recalling experiences of early childhood sexual abuse, will experience panic attacks, spiraling fear, sudden bouts of substance addiction, dissociative blackouts.

While I maintain a sympathetic and empathetic demeanor, some people may become defensive, guarded, suspicious, or fearful. They're projecting onto me the emotions they didn't allow themselves to feel earlier, in very vulnerable early life situations, where they began to suppress overwhelming feelings.

I encourage practitioners to not prepare what they want to talk about, but to speak entirely without a point or goal, sidestepping, as much as possible, the rigid narratives and perceptions they've constructed, to rely instead on spontaneous, emotion-based associations.

The emotional, relational parts of ourselves are used to being subjugated to our reasoning and self-justifications. But the truth does eventually emerge. When you or I draw or make a story up out of the blue, we're essentially revealing the emotional structures that subtly influence our perceptions of the world.

Practice:
Choiceless Awareness

Choiceless awareness is a practice in which we don't focus the mind on any particular aspect of our experience, but rather we maintain cognizance of how our attention moves from one object to another, then another, and so on. In essence we develop awareness of what we "keep in mind." This awareness can be achieved by labeling, or simply maintaining a detached awareness, so that we're observing the mind's "spotlight"—how our consciousness highlights certain objects or inner phenomena. For example, if we're replaying the interactions associated with a resentment, we simply note "resentment" or "remembering." We don't identify with thinking or any other mental process to the degree we can't observe how it works; we note how the mind is being used, how it's lured away from the present, how the workings of consciousness affect the body, feelings, breath.

Perhaps our attention will be drawn to body sensations or sounds or thoughts or to a mood such as calmness or sadness; perhaps we've experiencing a gut feeling in the belly, chest, or shoulders. Anything can be observed; the object is not important. What we're developing is an ingrained awareness: the recurrent, mechanical habit of constantly checking in to see how we're using the mind throughout the day. It's a relaxed practice, as we're not forcefully yanking our attention back to a phrase, or the breath, or the body, or emotions.

As this is a practice in which we don't choose an object, choiceless awareness integrates both conscious and unconsciously driven mental process. The left hemisphere, which tends to explicitly direct our attention toward socially useful goals,is asked to step back and allow the right hemisphere, which is often controlled by unconscious desires for security, connection, and often-buried impulses, to guide our attention. We learn a great deal by observing undirected attention.

To accomplish this practice we must maintain effort, for it takes practice, patience, and perseverance to maintain moment-to-moment awareness of the mind's direction. It's useful to keep in mind a clear, straightforward intention at the onset of this practice: I simply want to observe how my mind moves from one object to another: when it's jumpy, when it's settled. This means I'm not meditating to attain anything. I'm not seeking insight or tranquility; I'm just learning to observe the mind in action. Greed, anger, numbness, worry, anxiety, or self-doubt aren't hindrances in this practice; they're as valid as any other states of being to observe. I'm not attempting to get rid of uncomfortable sensations or dark moods. I'm cer-

Wisdom

WISDOM PUBLICATIONS

Please fill out and return this card if you would like to receive our catalogue and special offers. The postage is already paid!

NAME

ADDRESS

CITY / STATE / ZIP / COUNTRY

EMAIL

Sign up for our newsletter and special offers at wisdompubs.org

Wisdom Publications is a non-profit charitable organization.

tainly not judging anything. Again, it's not about getting rid of anything; it's simply observing what arises in consciousness.

Right now I'm sitting in a chair, looking away from my laptop to observe the idle wandering of my elderly cat; it's an unseasonably warm October afternoon, and my attention switches to the feeling of warm rays of sun flooding through the window. The feelings are pleasant, so it's easy to maintain an open mind to present-time experience. On some occasions I observe the world through perceptual biases—"I've got to get rid of that unpleasant sound," or "I really need to acquire that [insert electronic gizmo here]"— so my awareness begins to contract around objects that are either wanted or disliked.

Practicing choiceless awareness, in my experience, develops self-understanding, in which we learn about the tendencies that govern our mind's operation. This is as opposed to self-consciousness, the stifling tendency to judge and criticize our thoughts and impulses ("What will people think if I say this?"). Without any prejudice we observe our thoughts, feelings, emotions as processes; objects arise, the mind reacts, the objects pass, the flowing parade going on in the mind. Unlike self-consciousness, we're not trying to force the mind to produce thoughts and impulses that will be socially acceptable; so long as we maintain a detached observer, all thoughts and impulses can be useful to observe. I've spent my share of time observing how my attention bounces back and forth between resentment toward others and self-doubt. The more we develop our continuity of mindfulness, the more we can greet and hold any feeling or mood, no matter how unpleasant; we learn to be with them, rather than act out or repress them.

It's useful to keep the detached observer sharp and engaged by habitually asking questions: "What am I thinking about right now?" If the body becomes uncomfortable, or tired, or numb, we become interested in it, curious about it, turning toward the sensations and observing what they reveal.

◄ **III.**

Alone Together:
Connecting with Others

14. THE IMPORTANCE OF TRUE FRIENDS

THERE IS NO WAY to do spiritual practice alone—meditation is not enough. We must rely on true friends in order to do the work of being with others. Wise relationships with true friends help us to let go of self-centered perspectives.

We live in a society that revels in self-sufficiency and individuation. Popular culture celebrates autonomy and outsiders who "go it alone." In these narratives socialization is portrayed as a force that hems in freedom and creativity. By comparison dependence upon others is designated as weak or abnormal, even unhealthy.

It's not surprising—though a little dispiriting—that the term *codependency* has come to be taken so seriously and to be equated with the word "needy." It's not a clinical term; it was coined by members of Alcoholics Anonymous and popularized by Janet Woititz's *Adult Children of Alcoholics* to summarize the stifling results of alcoholic parenting. It refers to a kind of abuse, but it appears in pop culture as a demonized need for other human beings.

This cultural trait promotes a deeply flawed perspective on the human condition. Healthy relationships and mutual support are essential for psychological well-being. Our need for connection develops immediately in life; from infancy we learn to discern others' intentions and convey to them our needs. But we will never outgrow this need for others. Isolation, or even a series of failed attempts to connect with others, is psychologically painful and ultimately damaging. This is not conjecture: studies of people who have suffered from isolation—such as prisoners in solitary confinement and orphans who were poorly cared for—tells us that, without human connection, we will be damaged over the long term.

Focusing on the individual, rather than on our relationships, obscures our fundamental need for secure connection with others. We cannot coregulate—fully recognize and communicate for empathy and mirroring—our emotions in a vacuum.

A healthy individual self is developed via a network of relationships with other people. These relationships are internalized to provide self-compassion and self-care. Interactions with other people supply me with a psyche that is porous, in that I can absorb love from others. But this does not threaten my individual identity; rather, we mutually support one another's emotional resilience.

When we are unable to acknowledge and express underlying states of loneliness, we might binge-watch TV shows for distraction. Without support during times of anxiety or distress, we might bury ourselves in work or drown ourselves in a bottle. People who have been scarred by past relationships are primed to seek out drugs, alcohol, food, shopping, or workaholism as ways of avoiding their pain. Craving and addiction are often attempts to replace other people with substances: unsuccessful attempts to regulate emotions. The Buddha knew that treating our suffering requires secure connection with wise friends. This is why we take refuge not only in the Buddha and the Dharma, but also the Sangha, a community.

Despite the scientific and personal evidence of the necessity of relationships, for decades our culture has been separating us from one another. We no longer get together in squares and plazas to connect and talk for hours. Now we carry out our relationships online in the isolated comfort of our own homes. This might sound like an exaggeration, but research tells us that every hour we spend online will deprive us of a half hour of face-to-face conversation.

The process of connecting with others and synchronizing our moods is known as *attunement*, being seen and monitored by someone who cares about our happiness and security. It cannot occur via social media, though it is possible for it to be established via video calls such as Skype, Google Hangouts, and FaceTime. And yet despite how well psychologists have established intersubjectivity—our psychological dependence on one another to make sense of the world—our relational lives have become remarkably fragile. We're seeing the results in the escalating statistics of depression diagnosed in the United States.

To heal our losses and psychological wounds, we have to overcome our desire to replace others with habits and substances, and instead seek consistent, nurturing people who provide safe containers that can hold and manage such destructive impulses. Restoring our emotional regulation and healing our wounds can only be done by way of such healthy relationships. An essential element of spiritual practice is to locate other human beings who can help us break out of unhealthy cycles of alienation and isolation. If we are to become healthy human beings, we must find a community that provides nonjudgmental, open-hearted, empathetic alliances, where friends provide us with the support we need for continued growth.

Meditation and Community

Isn't meditation about internal focus and seclusion? Yes, but meditation is meant to be a part of a larger spiritual path that focuses on being with others. The Pali Canon has many more suttas detailing how to choose friends and act toward others than it has lessons concerning how to meditate. And remember: the Buddha informs us that wise friends are "the whole of the path" and "an essential foundation for the path."

It's only from connectedness that I can develop the capacity to be autonomous, not vice versa; only when my deepest need for attachment has been met can I handle the extended periods of seclusion I spend on retreat or in my daily meditation practice.

In contemporary Buddhism there is a potentially harmful trend to overemphasize meditation as the solution in and of itself. The idealization of long-term, silent retreats as the solution for suffering and despair is inappropriate and possibly harmful. While it is a valid endeavor for many practitioners, I've seen negative outcomes for people who have taken them when they were not well-prepared, such as just after a relationship ended or after the death of a loved one.

Over the years I've seen many people attempt to find peace during a week of silence without having first established meaningful support in the outside world. For many the sudden lack of contact results in an unhealthy state: lack of sleep, diminished appetite, repetitive ideations, anxiety, and panic attacks. In these cases, I've found it best to take them out of the silence and provide the dialogue and communication they need to temper the feelings that arise.

Of course I believe most people who are in a good place in life have the resources to handle themselves during week-long stints, where all forms of eye contact and communication are discouraged. Even people who are not in the best place in life can withstand the rigors of a silent retreat. Ideally, during a period of extended silence, we learn to sit with difficult emotions and triggering thoughts; through the practice, we develop a safe container for our internal states, from the pleasant to the disruptive.

But many practitioners will still struggle due to inner turmoil, and it important to know during such times of despair that what we need is an empathetic listener who allows us to voice our experience in a supportive environment. This helps to normalize and stabilize our experience. Since this is the case, it is apparent that silent meditation is not sufficient unto itself. In fact, in many situations it is a form of spiritual bypass. We may prefer meditation to the risk of developing true friendships. We will try isolating spiritual practices as a way past risking therapy or support groups.

Even in the practice of meditation, if we cannot make that safe container for ourselves, we still need the help of a teacher, or someone in the sangha to provide a reassuring emotional exchange. There is no way around our need to do the work together.

> A true friend gives what is hard to give, does what is hard to do. A good friend puts up with your mistakes and unfortunate words. A good friend tells secrets to you, while keeping yours safe. When misfortunes strike, a good friend doesn't abandon you or look down on you. When you locate someone so capable, put in all the effort needed to cultivate that friendship.

Practice:
Empathetic Connection

We support each other in the most lasting and meaningful way by listening and providing a stable, safe connection to each other's underlying emotions and feelings, rather than following the impulse to get caught up in details or judgments, to fix mistakes, to immediately agree or disagree with actions, etc.

So, what does empathetic connection look like?

(1) Direct your attention to someone and sustain it, putting aside all inner commentaries and distractions.

(2) Read the core emotional state that lies beneath their words. This requires focused attention: reading facial expressions, body language, listening to vocal inflections, etc.

(3) When a true connection occurs, open to any internal sensations that resonate with the feelings being signaled to you; empathy lies in the felt, not in the stories we add to a conversations.

(4) Listen without planning how to respond. Remind yourself that whatever emerges when it's your turn to speak should reflect what you feel, rather than offering advice, consolation, or feedback. We heal each other when we listen and mirror emotions, not though instructions.

(5) When it's time for you to speak, pause, feel, and know what is present before responding.

This is a practice of *mentalizing*, or locating the emotional states that lie beneath the stories and ideas the cognitive mind peddles as solutions. Details separate and isolate us, while feelings unite and connect; they are universally experienced. So even if there's conflict, or anger directed at you, ask "What are the feelings beneath his or her words? What am I feeling right now?" Simply responding with "I'm hearing that you're upset" can reduce tension more successfully than defending or explaining ourselves.

15. DEVELOPING GENUINE CONNECTION WITH OTHERS

UNPLEASANT EXPERIENCES are unavoidable. Rather than taking them personally, we can focus on their universality and combat suffering by keeping in touch with others, seeing and being seen by them, understanding their motivations, and having sympathy and empathy for them.

In Buddhism suffering is compared to two different types of arrows. The first arrow is the unpleasant experiences that are unavoidable: physical injury, sudden damage out of nowhere, old age, sickness, suffering, painful emotions, losing those we love and getting stuck with those we dislike. If we learn to accept such experiences as a natural part of existence, we can move through them more easily.

The second kinds of arrows occur when we are not particularly good at dealing with the bad news. We resist and refuse to take the bad with the good, though we certainly couldn't have one without the other. We would not have happy, positive feelings, if we did not have awful, negative ones with which to contrast them. Nonetheless, it's in our nature to enjoy the warm, sunny days while feeling cheated by cold and rainy patches. By resisting life's unpleasant experiences, we make them far more emotionally painful than necessary. The first kind of arrows life shoots at us. This second kind of arrow we shoot into ourselves.

How We Cause Ourselves Suffering

Denying the Inevitable

One of the forms those second arrows take is the deeply rooted human instinct to deny or resist the inevitable. We often think of this as adaptive—it's hard to forge ahead in life if we look only at inevitable doom—but it is very damaging when we are actually confronted with the inevitable. For example, many of us are not particularly happy about aging. Try as we might to face it with dignity, there are times when we deny our limitations—say, pushing ourselves to keep up with obligations despite bouts of sciatica, arthritis, and whatnot—which only makes matters worse. In the case of death, most people deny it just about every minute of every day simply by behaving as though it is nowhere in sight.

Something that is a more pressing concern, though, is our inclination to bypass the difficult conversations and interactions that our relationships require. If we spend meaningful time with family and friends, tensions will invariably arise and need to be addressed. This is also true of our relationship to our Buddhist community, teachers, and practitioners. At times these conversations are very welcome, but at others we'll feel an urge to avoid them and withdraw. When we do that, the result is loneliness, isolation, and invariably more conflict.

We Take Setbacks Personally

There is nothing particularly personal about the frustrating events of life. Missing the subway happens to everyone. Aging is what naturally happens to human bodies. However if we focus too much on how these things affect us, we tend to take them personally. The same goes for emotions—despite knowing how universal our feelings are, we experience our own frustration or loneliness as very unique and suspect that others won't understand. Asking ourselves "Why did this happen to me?" obscures the truth: life is a sequence of events in which we all sooner or later experience the unwanted and painful.

Early Buddhist commentaries tell the story of Kisa Gotami, a poor woman whose young child has died from a snake bite. Kisa cannot accept the tragedy, and so she carries her child's corpse around a village, asking people for medicine to revive her infant. Villagers, hoping to help her come to grips with the loss, direct her to the Buddha.

The Buddha, after hearing her story, explains that in order to receive the medicine she seeks, she must gather mustard seeds from a family in which no one has died.

As mustard seed is commonplace in India, Kisa excitedly runs from house to house; at first the occupants of each dwelling readily offer her the seeds, but when she asks if anyone in the family has died, the reply is always, "Why, yes . . ." Eventually the understanding sinks in: Loss and separation are universal experiences. This realization turns out to be the medicine the Buddha has promised: an understanding that life's blows are not personal affronts.

When we take life's slings and arrows personally, we lose awareness of the truth that binds us together and we isolate ourselves from the support of others. Seeing our feelings as unique makes it more difficult to share our emotional experiences with others. If we take bouts of depression personally, for example, we will fear that others might not understand if we talk to them about it, and we continue to feel isolated and suffer more.

Unfortunate events will continue to happen. But the Buddha gave us a reflection to counter these: "I will be parted from all I hold dear." Rather than taking events as a personal affront, we can remember the universality of the experience.

Failing to Recognize Impermanence

We have a very natural tendency, when thinking about nothing in particular, to speculate about and even attempt to predict the future. It makes sense. As the human brain was composed over the course of evolution, its dominant function was, of course, to help us thrive as a species and this required assimilating knowledge about various threats. So we have extremely fast neural pathways, which efficiently store a great deal of information about any perilous encounters or difficult experiences. Positive experiences, alas, tend to be stored by much slower memory circuits, so positive interpersonal events require far more time to be stored than negative ones. This is why we all have what's known as "negativity bias": in a relationship, for instance, we tend to remember the disappointing exchanges while overlooking the times a loved one checks in on us with a call or text. The relationship psychologist John Gottman's research showed that partners need five times as many positive interactions as negative for a relationship to be stable!

While one anecdote to negativity bias is to take time to soak in the positive moments of life, as a kind of counterbalance, another way to approach this disproportionate gravitation to the negative is to observe all experience as unfolding, in a constant flow. Both positive and negative experiences pass by.

Worrying What Other People Think

If we didn't worry so much about what others think of us, half our resentments would disappear. Once, decades ago, my twelve-step sponsor pointed this out to me and I immediately confirmed it by spending a great deal of time training myself to avoid speculating about how I'm perceived. It was difficult; my mind kept trying to pull me back into the guessing game. So I developed a simple training technique: Mondays, Wednesdays, Fridays, and Sundays I set aside for worrying about other people's opinions as much as my mind demanded; Tuesdays, Thursdays, and Saturdays were days when I would greet such thoughts and ask them to return on the following day, when they would be pondered, even entered into a journal. Eventually my brain's emotional circuits noted that I was just as safe in the world on the "no speculating about what others think" days as I was on other days; moreover the "no speculating" days were far more peaceful, with more time to focus on worthwhile thoughts and activities. The process took time but not much effort as I wasn't repressing thoughts; I was simply delaying them to agreed-upon days and times. I became much more relaxed. In fact, it's the only way I could possibly become a public speaker, which my Dharma teaching has demanded; I'm no more comfortable speaking in front of groups than most people. I've heard that the Buddha said, "There will be people who criticize you for talking too much, too little, and just the right amount." I'd like to believe this quote to be genuine, but I can't locate a record of it in the canon.

Avoidance, taking things personally, expecting the worst, and worrying about our reputations creates needless suffering. Fortunately we have our connection with each other to alleviate this suffering.

How to Connect with Others

Keeping in Touch (Maintaining Proximity)
Our social interactions are how we achieve safety: we survive in numbers, we are vulnerable alone. When we feel disconnected, we experience emotional pain. During hard times, we just want to feel close to others. When someone we love is nearby, we feel safer; it lightens whatever mood we're in.

Seeing Others and Being Seen by Them (Attunement)
Attunement is the ability to let somebody know that they are being seen, taken in, noticed; one thing I do in my mentoring

is to bring my glance back to meet another's glance in a way that they find predictable and reassuring. Being seen lets us explore the world, as we know someone has our back. It's easier for me to travel or walk into a new store or restaurant if my wife is with me, even though I'm perfectly safe without her. Having someone paying attention to us creates that needed security that allows for adventure and growth.

Sympathy

Sympathy is the ability to understand the story that somebody is conveying, the ability to stay present and to do our best to try to understand what is being presented. Sympathy, like proximity and attunement, asks that I focus attention away from inner chatter. If my attention is divided between what you're saying and preparing a response, I'll miss important cues you're sending me by way of your facial expression, body language, and tone. If I'm lost in thought, I'll fail to gather the emotions you express, and you'll sense that I've drifted away. Most people are naturally quite skilled at understanding when someone is paying attention. And whether they try to keep us interested in their story or change topics, that lack of attention doesn't help the person's process of communication, especially if they are trying to say something difficult or painful.

We listen to what is said, nodding to assure the other person that we understand the responsibilities and threats they're currently facing. Our role here is to intrude as infrequently as possible. We ask questions only when absolutely necessary to make sure we are following what the person is saying.

When it is time for us to speak, we have to fight off the impulse to fix or solve their problems, as the other person needs our solutions less than they need our sustained, receptive attention. If they need a suggestion, they'll tell us, but the urge to fix or solve is a sign that we're uncomfortable with what they're saying, that we need to get rid of the messiness of their emotions. It's not beneficial.

We also occasionally should check how we're breathing, whether our stomach is soft and shoulders relaxed. If we are physically tense, we have no room to take in another's experience. If we're stressed, we will feel an instinct to push away what they're sharing. We'll stiffen and they'll feel our resistance.

Understanding Motivations (Mentalization)

This is the same mentalization contained in the practice at the end of chapter 14. Mentalization is the ability to reflect and understand the underlying mental states that motivate another person's thoughts and behavior, to understand what they mean, even if their words don't accurately convey what they're attempting to convey. This is a profoundly important skill. Without mentalization we fail to understand irony, play, or even that someone may have hidden intentions that differ greatly from what they state. We learn this through practice, by holding and reflecting all the signals another sends. Nonverbal expressions can indicate intentions that are entirely at odds with what is being spoken.

Empathy

Empathy is our ability to feel, internally, what somebody else is feeling. Empathy is similar to mentalization—they overlap in many ways—in that it involves discerning another person's subtle, even latent or veiled emotions. Empathy differs from mentalization in that it involves little thought or cognition; it's based on sensing what another person experiences. When someone we are with is sad, we will feel the affect within us as well, in our bodies, faces, and mood. Though we do not likely feel the emotion as strongly as the other person, we reflect their joyful or painful feelings, which helps them to process those emotions.

Empathy is a very challenging proposition. If it is done well, it communicates that a person is not alone. It unconsciously conveys to each of us that we understand one another's state of being, which alleviates our feelings of isolation.

The downside of empathy is emotion contagion: we can be easily "brought down" by others. When we encounter someone who is suffering, though we may have just been upbeat and cheerful, we may fall into their mood and afterward feel as sad and despairing as they were. Experiencing painful emotion contagion can even create an impulse within us to avoid people or emotional situations altogether, which is not helpful to ourselves or others.

For this reason it is important to remember this: taking on another's suffering is not part of the plan. Breathing in the suffering of others only works if we breathe it out as well. Hanging on to the moods of others will leave us spent and exhausted, especially if we work in the caring professions.

ALONE TOGETHER: CONNECTING WITH OTHERS

How to Take Care of Others by Taking Care of Ourselves

Working with others takes both patience and practices that rinse away the distress and agitation we encounter throughout the day. It requires a lot of courage to sit, listen, and allow friends or loved ones to express and signal painful states without trying to solve or get rid of what they are feeling. As caring people, how can we be present for others who are suffering without becoming so involved that we wind up suffering ourselves?

Practice:
The Long Exhalation

It's helpful to relax the body and breath while we are around someone who is suffering. Make the belly soft and the shoulders relaxed and then just make the out-breath very long. We can still be open and present to them. We can still take in what they are communicating, still sympathize, and still attune to them.

Rather than distracting us, the breathing and relaxation will actually help us to not absorb their tension and to not get caught up in our own internal chatter. If our bodies are relaxed when others present their painful feelings to us, we will have a container that can hold it so that we are not completely overrun. But if we are tense and resistant, we will either not be able to feel them, or we will mirror the painful feelings they are projecting.

Practice:
Labeling the Emotion

Sometimes, when working with people who are affected by strong emotions, it can be very helpful to have them name the mental state they're experiencing. Labeling aloud helps other people identify what emotion they are experiencing, of which they might be totally unaware. This practice calls attention to the emotion that's being presented, which helps me detach and gain a healthy distance. I can still empathize, but I won't become overly involved in their narrative.

Practice:
Cleansing Ritual Practice

There is a ritual meditation that I do after my last one-on-one interview and before I move on to the rest of the evening. If I don't take an inventory of myself and my feelings, I find that I'll carry with me other people's moods.

The most effective tool for this kind of self-inventory is the body scan. What this entails is lying down somewhere comfortable and scanning, or feeling the internal sensations in each area of the body, starting from the top of the head and gradually moving down. Wherever we sense muscle contraction or numbness, we pause and use the breath to restore, as much as possible, those areas to a state of ease. This way, we systematically cleanse our bodies of any stray tension that may have accumulated.

Balance

In Buddhism, equanimity (or *upekkha* in Pali) is a wisdom tool that provides checks and balances for kindness, compassion, and appreciation. We will experience those who are suffering in ways we cannot alleviate, no matter how great our resources and empathy. We need enough awareness to avoid getting caught up in trying to help to the point that we create needless frustration and stress, both for them and for us. As one great teacher, the monk Ajahn Geoff, so frequently notes, equanimity is the factor that allows us to redirect our efforts where we *can* be of use. So equanimity isn't insensitive, but rather it knows when our compassion is wasted and where it should be guided instead.

What allows us to redirect our attention from suffering we cannot help is discernment: some suffering arises over a significant period of time, over a long course of maladaptive coping strategies or self-sabotaging addictions, and the resulting emotional states are too much for us to address. We may be able to employ a wide variety of sound healing practices, but we cannot rescue everyone, in the same way that a doctor cannot cure certain diseases. Just as we would not want a doctor to be emotionally torn apart by such cases, so should we not allow ourselves to be torn apart by their emotional equivalents. We cannot let our desire to help others make us butt our heads against invisible brick walls and ultimately cause us suffering. When we do this, we have really just added one more suffering person to the world. Many people are easily ensnared in caretaking quagmires with friends or family members. This doesn't indicate that those people are somehow weak. Even therapists with decades of experience find themselves struggling with certain types of patients. As an old saying goes, sometimes it's more likely that the drowning person will pull you out of the boat than that you'll pull them to safety.

16. CULTIVATING A SMART HEART

WHEN WE CULTIVATE goodwill toward all beings, we feel compassion for them when they suffer and empathetic joy for them when they are happy, and we treat them all with equanimity. But we should be smart in our development of these attitudes, taking different personality types into consideration when considering how best to begin.

No book on the Buddhist practice of insight is complete without an explanation of the special virtues, or states known as *brahmaviharas*. Translated alternately as the "sublime attitudes," "divine abodes," or "four immeasurables," the brahmaviharas are states of limitless goodwill, compassion, empathetic joy, and equanimity.

These are heartfelt intentions cultivated from positive emotions and attitudes with which we already have experience. Since each of them is a state that we have in relation to other people, we can best cultivate them by drawing on those times that we connect happily with friends and loved ones, with feelings of love and care.

Metta is the wish that all beings, including myself, will achieve happiness due to the skillfulness of my actions. When we cause harm to others, even in small ways, such as not returning a phone call, we tend to either feel a sense of shame or begin generating justifications. In either case our minds become agitated. It's far easier, in the long term, to be benevolent and caring, and the result is a much more tranquil mind. Extending this kind of goodwill replaces all of that chaotic self-reflection with the simple wish that everyone will benefit from my skillful actions. Our wish for everyone's peace of mind becomes the source of our own peace of mind.

When someone who's developed goodwill chances upon suffering, the natural response is to feel the next brahmavihara: compassion. Compassion (*karuna*) is the desire to see suffering relieved, either in myself or another being. But how does this compassion manifest into action? When we see that someone we care about is suffering, we can't merely wish them happiness, nor should we help them to take the bait that brings them only fleeting happiness. Rather, compassion demands that we show them that they don't need to suffer. Compassion prompts us to take action to alleviate their suffering, by giving them care and teaching them self-care. We help give them a safe container for their painful feelings and when it is appropriate, we give them space.

Goodwill and compassion lie at the heart of spiritual practice. According to the *Ayacana Sutta*, after the dawn of his enlightenment, the Buddha spent a period of days beneath the bodhi tree, in a state of pure equanimity and selfless perception. Because he knew that the Dharma is hard for people driven by craving—us—to understand, he hesitated to teach it at all.

> There's no point teaching what was so difficult for me to attain. This Dhamma is too difficult to understand by those motivated by aversion and passion.

For people driven by greed and fear, the Dharma is a hard sell. In this sutta and elsewhere in the Pali Canon, it is often said to be "against the stream" of the world.

Fortunately, the story goes, at this moment the Buddha was visited by a god named Sahampati. The deity was alarmed to find that the Buddha had lost his motivation to teach:

> The world has been deprived of its safekeeper! For the Awakened One is dwelling in peace, not roaming about, teaching the Dhamma . . . Rise up, victorious, awakened one! Teach what you've learned to others, though you owe no debt to the world. For there will be those who will understand your insights.

The Buddha considered this request and, as he felt compassion for all beings, was ultimately convinced to teach the Dharma because he saw that there were other people he had met who would benefit from it. Motivated by goodwill, he covered thousands of miles by foot, offering his insights for free, when he could have just sat there under a tree, enjoying his own exalted state. When he offered his second discourse, the *Anatta Lakkhana*, five other practitioners immediately experienced awakening; subsequently untold thousands achieved awakening, as his talks drew increasingly greater audiences.

Empathetic joy (*mudita*) is what someone practicing goodwill feels when they meet others who are experiencing joy and secure connections. It is the emotional response we feel for somebody who has worked diligently, without resorting to duplicitous means, and is enjoying the fruits of their actions. We live in a competitive society, so it's easy to be envious when someone feels joyous and we do not. But others' happiness does not deprive us of our own; there is plenty of happiness to go around. It is important to be able to appreciate happiness when it's merited in order to transcend the petty competitiveness of our capitalist society that drives us through greed and endless craving.

Equanimity (*upekkha*) is the internalization of a balanced attitude. Equanimity is a counterbalance to the pulling of our passions in one direction or another. It helps us to see and understand without being unduly influenced by our own craving. But this is still relational; when people that we care about are suffering, equanimity allows us to see them and help them without being pulled into their suffering. This is a very powerful tool for helping others. If you needed surgery, would you really want a surgeon who feels everything their patients feel? Not only would they bring all of their previous patients' agony into your surgery with them, they would have to work through yours, as well. It may seem like an extreme analogy, but it is accurate. Without equanimity, we are like the blind leading the blind.

It's quite easy to detach emotionally from people we don't know well or don't immediately care about. It's harder, on the other hand, to feel equanimity with those we love. So equanimity is a practice that changes depending upon how close we feel with the recipient.

A Twist on the Usual Teachings

Generally teachers instruct that the brahmaviharas should be practiced as much as possible. This guidance makes sense if we assume that people all have the same psychological makeup. If we were uniform in demeanor, essentially secure, and emotionally regulated, it would make sense for each of us to go forth and practice goodwill, compassion, empathetic joy, and equanimity wherever it seems appropriate.

But human beings don't arrive with uniform mental states, degrees of emotional regulation, or interpersonal skills. All of the brahmavihara tools don't fit all practitioners all the time. It's worth taking some time to discern which tools we need to practice with greater effort in certain relationships, and which tools are best put aside for the time being. How can we apply these suitably for different types of people?

If We Feel Secure in Relationships

Securely attached adults tend to be confident in the durability of their relationships. These individuals were fortunate to have, in their earliest years, caretakers who were attentive, tolerant, and mirroring. In these first stages of nonverbal bonding, the infant's parents or gaurdians provided a secure base: the child knew there was a safe place in the world where it could expect protection and care, and so they could venture out into the world, make new connections, explore. The secure adult has a similar connection with their partner, in that they feel significant others are reliable and available, which provides the confidence to explore life as fully as possible.

Secure adults don't run from requests for intimacy and attention, nor seek constant attention, for they don't harbor constant expectations of abandonment or rejection; early life experiences have instilled confidence in relationships. These individuals are honest with their needs, balance work obligations with family commitments, can develop independent interests and friendships while maintaining a robust intimacy with their partner. Often, when meeting with secure practitioners, I tend to empathize cultivating compassion for the suffering of others; they can find the self-sabotaging behaviors of anxious and avoidant individuals to be mystifying. The strength of their early attachments can make the insecurity of others difficult to fathom.

If We Feel Anxious in Relationships

Those who are anxious in relationships struggle to express their needs as clearly, as they expect to be disappointed. They feel safer beating around the bush, hinting at their needs, for even though being vague about one's wants increases the risks of disappointment, they feel safer not asking outright, for to be rejected when they've taken the risk of vulnerably disclosing their desire feels too emotionally painful.

So in a situation in which a secure person might tell us "Hey, it's my birthday and I'm having some people over; I'd like you to come," a very anxious person might simply say "So, it's my birthday on Friday." They'll only hint, as though other people should intuit their desires and intentions. If we cannot, they might become agitated or ruminate over the interaction, becoming increasingly bothered by the disappointing outcome, which was ultimately brought about by their indirectness.

As a consequence, insecure people are alternately too tolerant in relationships or, ironically, completely intolerant. On one hand they are always willing to drop their boundaries in order to keep a relationship that they want, but on the other, they are likely to flee when they feel the pain that comes from not getting their needs met.

People who are anxious in relationships should go about the brahmaviharas in a very specific way. If fixating on a particular person with whom they want a relationship is their default, then practicing goodwill and compassion might provide them with a spiritual-sounding excuse to ruminate. Instead, developing equanimity in that relationship should be a first priority. A mind that obsessively flows toward any object must be patiently restrained through practice.

Once some equanimity is achieved, we should develop goodwill toward everyone else in our lives, beyond the person with whom we are preoccupied. When we are focused on just one relationship, our anxious minds have little care or concern for other people. Yes, we might claim to be caring, and we might have caring feelings in the background, but these objections are deceptive. While we are fixated on one person, everyone else receives little sincere, attuned attention. So it's very important when we're in this circumstance to remember all of the other beings deserving of attention and care.

Also important to note: self-compassion is very important for those stuck on one relationship. When we are caught up in the drama of a relationship and do not feel compassion for ourselves, it is worthwhile to acknowledge that we are suffering, to pull our attention away from what the other is doing, to see how much we are suffering by fixating on this one thing.

If We Feel Avoidant in Relationships

Almost the exact antithesis to those who are anxious in relationships are those who are avoidant. These are individuals who found their parents or caretakers to be either emotionally inscrutable or engulfing/smothering, and so as adults they prioritize self-reliance, with an inclination to retreat when emotional intimacy is sought. The primary inclination in this state is to pull away and keep a safe remove.

Experiencing life with the expectation of engulfment, with little if any faith in the value of intimacy in romantic relationships, these individuals do not need to focus on developing boundaries in relationships, as they are already detached from the relationship, almost indifferent. When anxious partners seek a greater degree of relational commitment, they are viewed as needy, perhaps overly demanding. Those with avoidant tendencies occasionally hold up a single, past partner as the "one that got away," in comparison to which all others fall short. I've listened to many individuals who fit this pattern, and I've found the callous disregard they feel for sexual partners to be, at times, astonishing. One young male practitioner informed me that he was finished with a woman he slept with on a few occasions. When I inquired as to what led to this decision, he explained she was "crowding him,"—she'd had the temerity to wish him a happy birthday (which it was)! In short, I often find it necessary to remind avoidants that no one deserves suffering, and people aren't "needy" simply for having needs.

Those who feel this way often in relationships will benefit from developing the basic metta themes of goodwill and compassion. To address the inclination to flee or pull away from others, it's useful to cultivate an understanding that all beings deserve love, care, tolerance, support.

It's Never As Simple As It Seems

Attachment styles should not be thought of as a pathology or diagnosis; they can significantly change over time and life experiences. An individual with anxious tendencies can gravitate toward a secure attachment if they chose a partner—or therapist—who is empathetic, reliable, attentive during interactions. Furthermore, over the course of a lifetime, just about all of us will express, at one time or another, assured, anxious, and avoidant approaches to our interpersonal connections. We might use each approach in different relation-ships, or even the two styles in the same relationship. But if we deeply reflect on our core inclinations when we feel vul-nerable in a relational setting—to seek assurance, keep our distance, or calmly work things out—we may well find that we tend to fall into one of these categories more than oth-ers. It is my experience that if we understand the underlying patterns and tendencies, the greater the likelihood we can lastingly alleviate behaviors that cause us, or others, harm.

Practice:
Equanimity

Sit in a balanced posture and close your eyes, if that is comfortable for you. Bring a receptive attention to your breath, or the ambient sounds of the space you're in, until your mind starts to settle and your heartbeat seems slower.

Begin by reflecting on the benefits of achieving spiri-tual balance in life. What is it like to fully open to and feel each moment, yet remain free of reactivity, judg-ment, any desire to get rid of or cling to an experi-ence? See if you can open to—from the lower body up, gradually, to the head—a state of ease that is not guarded or armored.

Reflect on how all of our feelings and emotional states appear then disappear. All life arises and passes in waves, moments of serenity and agitation, happiness and sadness. Just try to sit calmly through that parade of experience. Say, "May I be with all of my experience with peace and ease; may I receive all of life and open to it."

Finally remember that each of us lives in the results of our actions, that joy and distress is created by actions. We cannot lastingly alleviate the suffering of others, only guide them to the path, where they must take the steps. Repeat three times: "May I know what needs to be done; may I do it; may I learn from the results."

17. CULTIVATING WISE FRIENDSHIPS

WE REVEAL OURSELVES incrementally to friends to discover those to whom we can speak openly and honestly about our struggles, without fear of judgment. Wise friends reflect us with grace and tolerance and help us understand ourselves: they do what is hard to do.

Sharing or processing our emotions is an essential, irreplaceable role that wise friends fill in our lives. In the *Upadda Sutta*, the Buddha says,

> Wise friends and camaraderie is the whole of the spiritual life.

And in the *Sambodhi Sutta*:

> With admirable friends you will know how to act with virtue, listen and speak well, persist on the path and acquire wisdom.

From the moment we are born, none of us can survive alone. In addition to our physical needs, the core of our emotional lives is essentially our connection to and ability to share with others. When we interact, we are unconsciously trying to signal to others our state of being, seeking a response. Humans cannot regulate emotions alone.

The Commodification of Relationships

Given how necessary genuine emotional connection is to our well-being, it's alarming to note how free-market values have encroached into our intimate relationships. As Tinder, OkCupid, Facebook, etc., are now integral parts of meeting, friendship, and romance, we now treat other human beings and our relations the same way that we treat commodities. When we meet someone face-to-face at a party, we interact with them and get to know them organically, unconsciously processing all of the information they give us, not only by their words, but by their gestures and expressions, even their pheromones. We would have to go to great lengths to deny that they are a real person. On an app on our phone, we look over a person's pictures (packaging), their basic description (product features), and select them or not, like we pick out a pair of sneakers. We can buy a pair today, knowing we can always throw them away in a few weeks and run back to the market for a new pair.

Instead of viewing them as our necessary companions, we increasingly view friends as sources of entertainment and lovers as providers of sensual pleasure. Unfortunately, the amount of sensual gratification or entertainment any human being can provide another is ultimately ephemeral. If a connection with another being is based primarily on the entertainment or distraction it provides, the relationship is like candy; it tastes good but it won't nurture or sustain us.

If we grow accustomed to thinking about relationships in this way, the anonymity and consumerism without risk and vulnerability will breed impatience. The delusion of limitless possibilities will undermine our ability to commit, for we'll believe that out there, in the world, better options are available.

It creates a delusion that, given the right choice, we will wind up with a relationship—platonic or romantic—that isn't challenging, that doesn't require patience and compromise to sustain, and that's simply not realistic. Authentic affiliations aren't easy, they require the practice of a thousand conversations and acts of forgiveness to build up the security and confidence required to make it work. Relationships just don't feel good every day; there are periods where we test each other's patience, which only makes our bonds more secure.

Consumerism breeds the belief that we deserve nothing but a smooth, ideal conclusion to every choice we make. This may be available in footwear, but not in human beings.

If we're looking for an ideal match, disappointment is the inevitable outcome. What excites and satisfies us in the short term is quite often not ultimately beneficial or sustainable. But even a very suitable relationship won't survive if we are dead set on finding an ideal match. Comparing an actual relationship against an ideal, the actual will lose every time. The ordinary frustrations and misunderstandings of normal relationships can make even a perfect match feel unbearable. Commonplace challenges begin to seem like impositions rather than opportunities to develop closeness, forgiveness, and improved communication skills.

Also, thinking that life will be simpler with someone else obscures the fact that we tend to choose the same sorts of relationships time and time again, finding ourselves in the same situations; the faces may change, but the challenges remain the same.

Risking Relationship

Commitment and intimacy ask us to make countless decisions: how and when to make bids for attention, how to respond, how to express feelings, how to provide genuine assurance, rather than relying on hollow words, roses, boxes of chocolate, and greeting cards. True connection rests on an ability to invest in a path, a secure relationship that withstands the momentary bumps along the journey. Happiness comes from meaningful connection, which is not born of momentary episodes but of sustained emotional presence.

If we can't risk making meaningful connections with others, we will miss out on intimacy, genuine disclosure, and vulnerability. Expressing our most concealed yearnings or feelings of shame is as crucial as it is hazardous, for rejection will sting the most when we dare to communicate what we've suppressed. Doubt and hesitancy provide the perfect opportunity to avoid intimacy. Even being the first to say "I like you" in person can feel terrifying to someone in the habit of connecting by text messages and Facebook posts. Given the complexity of meaningful relationships that involve the vulnerability of phone calls and face-to-face interactions, learning how to negotiate the unavoidable conflicts of relational experience are skills that relatively few people master. The consequence of becoming intimacy-averse is a profound sense of isolation and disconnection.

On the other hand not all relationships are meant to endure. Priorities shift in individuals: some might become involved in spiritual pursuits, others engaged by worldly careers. After significant life events, our needs for attention and care can reveal incompatibilities. In some cases the rifts can be so sudden that feelings of abandonment or rejection arise. Certainly any relationship containing verbal or physical abuse, or any of the often-subtle variations of shaming, may not be worth salvaging. Resilience and effort should be employed only toward those ties that are nontoxic.

A spiritual practice, though, requires properly balancing our efforts, focusing less on choosing the right partner, while investing more effort into providing a secure connection for those who are in our lives. The challenge of tolerance, pausing, and seeking to understand the underlying mental states that motivate the behavior of others requires that we learn how to set aside our self-centered perspectives, which so often lead to holding grudges, competing for recognition, or settling scores.

A support group provides the most reliable of all human connections. While even the most trustworthy individuals can let us down should they face stressful challenges, a support group, such as a spiritual community or twelve-step program, provides access to enough individuals that we can feel reliably supported if we know how to reach out for guidance. This is why the Buddha so constantly emphasized "wise spiritual friends" as the bedrock of the path. A community offers a setting where I can "right size" my feelings of loneliness, failure, fear. When I get together with other teachers in the Against the Stream community, I can voice the challenging experiences of being a Dharma teacher: the financial precariousness of living by donations, the stresses of teaching the Dharma, etc.

Discerning Wise Friends

We can engage our relationships as spiritual practice by opening up to spiritual growth through our connection with others. In teachings to lay practitioners, the Buddha expresses helpful insights into how we can make smart choices in relationships. Mostly the focus is on how to discern wise, spiritual friends and how to go about developing relationships with them skillfully. The Buddha was not only presenting a path to ultimate enlightenment, but also a blueprint for developing interpersonal connections that heal emotional wounds and traumas.

This practice of discerning wise friends implies that there are other kinds of friends, unreliable or unhelpful ones. The work of connecting with others involves risk. In order to mend and grow spiritually, we have to be able to get past disappointment and abandonment. As we open our hearts, some people will recoil because, perhaps, they have no room in their lives for anyone else's suffering. Other people may stay, but not be beneficial to our path. Our task is to persevere and find those who will receive us with grace and tolerance. To do this we need to build up our sense of security; no one risks authenticity while feeling scared.

Though we may have been disappointed by past relationships, we certainly can't give up on making true connections. Security cannot be achieved by sealing ourselves off from others. It's a dire outcome if I give up being open, vulnerable, and expressing my sadness or fears with others, choosing to shut down my inner states via drugs, alcohol, food, or other addictions.

Over the last decade, I have had the privilege to do lots of spiritual mentoring. Through this I've developed strategies to help people build a secure base with other people so that they feel more secure as they gradually open up to others. I offer it to you here.

Incremental Revealing

The first principle is to reveal ourselves incrementally: if we open up too quickly or haphazardly, or if we prematurely disclose our most vulnerable feelings, we open ourselves up to being wounded again. We need to be conscious about how we develop intimate friendships, how we move into new relationships. It's worthwhile to open up gradually, in order to naturally maintain a sense of safety.

Almost all of us have experienced painful abandonments,

rejections, shaming. So, as we make new friends, it is useful to think of it as moving through stages, starting from not knowing someone, to becoming intimate friends. Most people have around one hundred and fifty casual acquaintances, a smaller group of around fifty people that are friends, and an even smaller inner circle of five people that are a close support group—people that are the type of reliable friends that the Buddha says form the foundation of the spiritual life. The stages of friendship I use essentially move us through these circles, from the outermost one hundred fifty, to the innermost five.

This might seem a bit calculated, but building relationships with others without incremental boundaries leads to self-sabotaging results.

The First Stage: Getting to Know You

To become acquaintances we must first get to know one another. We tell each other the details of our day and come to be friendly enough to have casual but not intimately detailed conversations. We share a glimpse of our lives, but nothing too daring or revealing. At this point we're in our outermost circle, the people who are acquaintances and colleagues. We care enough to share some events from our lives and make some connection, but we don't risk very much. Still, just being seen has an emotional value.

The Second Stage: Taking a Small Risk

Next we take a small risk in order to develop our friendship. We share with each other the frustrations and disappointments we experience in life. It's easy to share triumphs, but disappointments involve a greater degree of vulnerability. In this step we begin to test the waters and see if our friend can be trusted with something that is difficult for us.

It's very important that I move from step one to step two and not go too far too fast. If we move too quickly and reveal too much, we'll probably catch our friend off guard by revealing too much information.

The Third Stage: Taking a Bigger Gamble

Then we take a bigger gamble, sharing feelings that require greater vulnerability and trust. We move into a new stage of friendship by disclosing those more personal, difficult, and less obvious feelings. Rather than just frustrations, we might open up about our deeper fears and concerns in life. By offering these feelings to others, we have an opportunity to evaluate how prepared our friend is to connect. He or she might contradict our feelings, or try to be reassuring. They might express a genuine interest, or try to solve the problem for us. If we communicate our needs well and the other person persists in giving advice or subtly judging or shaming us, we can take it as a sign that we should shift back to stage one. If over time our friend proves to be capable of holding our difficult emotions, we can move on to the deepest stage of friendship.

The Fourth Stage: The Wise Friend

At this stage, the person is now a part of my inner circle, the trusted five or six people on whom I can reliably depend to help me regulate difficult internal states; additionally, I can share with you my most painful experiences. The wise friend is someone with whom we can share the impulses or experiences with which we truly struggle, the kind that we don't generally reveal unless we feel completely safe. We don't want to reveal our deepest secrets to just anyone.

Having someone with whom we can share our harmful feelings and actions is very good for our spiritual growth. By talking with them, we can come to understand the nature of our harmful cycles. The Buddha said to his son, Rahula:

> If you act in a way that causes self-harm, to the harm of others, or to both, then it was an unskill-ful act. You should reveal it to a spiritual teacher or to a wise friend. Having admitted the act, it will help you exercise restraint in the future.

Now, while we'll always need to have a small, core inner circle of friends, the people who comprise this group can change. Some people we trust today may become unavailable in a few years, for a variety of reasons. It's just the way of life. So we have to take it upon ourselves to reach out to new people and explore where we can find support in the future. Everything is impermanent, even wise friendships.

Also when we find that a close friend is suddenly unavailable, or we've had a few disappointing encounters, don't push them out of your life. Simply take them down to a safer level of vulnerability. It's essential, if we are to develop a sense of security in the world, to avoid black-and-white strategies such as latching onto people then dropping them completely.

Setting Secure Boundaries

It would be foolish to talk about developing new intimate friendships without putting in a few words about boundaries. While there are the stages that should govern how quickly I move into a new relationship, I'll also need to maintain a set of rules governing which actions, conversational topics, and situations I'm willing to engage in with someone. These are rules based on my experience of behaviors that are unsafe.

At the very least, they should comprise what in Buddhist practice we call the five precepts, namely, refraining from killing, stealing, harmful speech, irresponsible sex, or intoxication. Beyond those, we will have our own, very personal boundaries—or rules—that we uphold in our relationships. We maintain secure boundaries in order to safely put ourselves into vulnerable situations. Knowing that we have measures in place to keep us secure, we can allow ourselves to be less guarded and vigilant. It's up to each of us to discern and construct our boundaries based on our individual needs; what makes me feel safe in the world might leave you vulnerable; your needs may make me feel confined, etc.

It is also important to note that boundaries constitute a personal code of ethical behaviors, which I need not justify or defend. They're not laws or social policies I'm willing to debate. No one can compel me to defend my boundaries. Falling into that trap, we will find them quickly eroded.

In many ways boundaries define the difference between how childhood and adults interact with others. Children exist in power dynamics wherein they cannot easily set boundaries; most children would struggle to say to a parent or teacher, "I'm not ready to discuss my plans for the future, as I find you to be overbearing and, frankly, intolerant of my core goals." Deprived of the necessary ability to set secure guidelines to govern relationships, children often rely on extreme strategies to survive family and educational systems: people-pleasing at all costs, perfectionism, avoidance coping, narcissistic attention-seeking, excessive caretaking, hypervigilance. These strategies, born of the need to maintain a secure connection with adults, will in time become ingrained, maladaptive behaviors that sabotage our ability to authentically connect with others.

Adult boundaries, conversely, help us connect authentically; we can express our core feelings, needs for intimacy or space, and goals and desires without fear of abuse or extreme rejection. With boundaries, we are willing to state that we will not participate in any conversation if we are interrupted, ridiculed, insulted, exposed to contempt, eye-rolling, stonewalling, yawning, looking away. We can insist that those we converse with must repeat back to us our statements without alteration (a form of mirroring) before expressing their own views, as we will repeat their words back to them. We can set time limits to conversations, insist that others be present to insure proper conduct; we are allowed to rule out certain locations in order to feel safe.

Staying Calm While the Bullets Whiz Overhead

All relationships involve some periods of conflict, times when our needs just don't sync up smoothly. We may reach out to a friend for reassurance and find they are busy, or need time to relax. Someone might want you to see his or her band play in some remote neighborhood and you may decline. All meaningful relationships will have times when people are not being heard, not getting their needs met, or feeling disappointed. It is hard for each of us to get our needs met when we are counting on each other to help.

In my experience with working with relational conflicts, there are often a number of buried psychological issues at play that sustain discord between lovers, friends, family members. Mundane, present-day interactions, such as petty conflicts and small disappointments, may feel disproportionately unacceptable as they've stirred up earlier wounds that haven't been properly addressed, grieved, healed. For instance, sometimes I find myself outraged by criticism: My partner Kathy notes how loudly I close doors, and I feel a surge of heat flow up my chest to my face. My arms tense. Why is this so embittering for me? It's activating the old, unexpressed anger I felt toward my father who, at times, would criticize my every step. As a child it didn't feel safe to voice indignation to a drunk adult who towered over me, so I pushed the emotions down. As a result, today criticism can be triggering if I don't pause, breathe, and process the energy mindfully, before proceeding to acknowledge my actions, discuss, or even calmly debate the appropriate way to close doors.

Often the behavior I find most irritating in others seems intolerable because it's similar to impulses or emotions I've repressed to survive in the world. As an example, to engage with other boys throughout my teens, I learned to rely on humor, verbal banter, or consuming copious amounts of booze and weed—comportments that came to me naturally. I disavowed any urges to be laid back and cool, for if I attempted to appear aloof and thoroughly detached, similar to vintage Lou Reed or Bob Dylan, I actually came across as ludicrous. People would roll their eyes—my social anxiety settings are simply set too high to pull off being aloof. Since I abandoned any impulses toward acting reserved and casual, I find other men who are emotionally unresponsive to be irritating; they're acting out what I've pushed down by force. So those who present themselves as cold-blooded make my blood boil. The same goes for aggressive or macho behavior, which I've long suppressed—if I ever had any to begin with.

I've found that conflicts are far easier to resolve when I take to heart the core Buddhist insight into the subjective quality of all views, opinions, and thoughts. (The *Dhammapada* reminds us that everything we experience occurs in a mind, and all minds have biases and prejudicial qualities.) Rather than regarding a critical colleague's assessments as inciting, if I open to the possibility that their point of view might actually contain a glimmer of truth or, gulp, real insight into my maladaptive behaviors, there is possibility for self-understanding and growth. If I instinctively defend myself rather than reflect, there is little possibility for deepening understanding between myself and another individual.

On several past occasions Noah Levine confronted me in teachers' meetings about topics about which I harbor rather unyielding views—for example, a dismissiveness toward the idea of rebirth, which I find preposterous. I find that if I take time to reflect on his comments, rather then immediately become defensive, they often point to areas where I'm pedantic, even unreasonable.

The experience born of teacher training, Buddhist mentoring, and therapy, not to mention fifteen years of marriage, have taught me that virtually every criticism I receive—*especially if it stings*—offers some glimmer of perceptive truth. Now and then stressed-out truck drivers have hurled random insults at me, as they seem to find bicyclists a nuisance that shouldn't be allowed access to city streets. The abuse never leaves a lasting emotional wound, as the words contain no truth; they don't know me, so nothing hits a sore spot. But my wife's sideswipes invariably rattle around in my mind—there's invariably more than a kernel of insight in them. Once, in the midst of a flare-up concerning when the timing would be best to paint our bedroom, Kathy called me a "prima donna," which lingered for days, as it no doubt contained real perception into the self-righteous views I was voicing.

The Greatest Cause of Conflict Is Avoidance

Quite often conflict avoidance is the secret culprit to ongoing tension in our relationships. Many of us will go to great lengths to navigate around necessary confrontations, wherein we either acknowledge our own disappointments or the disappointments of others, with a romantic partner, friend, colleague, or family member. Of course, sidestepping potentially stressful interactions doesn't make conflict go away. In failing to address disagreements or frustrations, conflict goes underground in relationships, seeping everywhere—like garbage improperly buried, its pollution doesn't stay put—making every small interaction with a loved one rife with tension. Or we may expend a great deal of time and effort to avoid contact with people who activate anger or embarrassment, but all that accomplishes is adding greater resistance to working through issues.

To illustrate: Neither of my parents ever acknowledged my proliferation of tattoos, though they were certainly quite apparent during their lifetimes. My mother would look away from my arms—she found them unspeakable—while my father would survey the designs on my neck and hands yet fail to utter a word—derisive, as I'd expect from him, or otherwise. I responded in kind, never addressing the art creeping over the surface of my body; I felt the presence of the unacknowledged in many of our interactions, and it created a sense of artificiality to some of the last, precious times we connected.

Avoiding conflict that might result from speaking with truthful and appropriate intentions isn't spiritual; it's simply cowardly. The wise don't avoid conflicts.

When motivated by noble goals, such as acknowledging underlying tensions or setting boundaries, the sensible directly address issues, seeking appropriate resolutions. Naturally, if we have histories of relational wounds inflicted in childhood, we'll find expressing our needs to be frightening; our impulses and intuitions will guide us in the wrong direction, to navigate around direct, straightforward interactions. If we follow these evasive inclinations and suppress them, eventually the pent-up anger and disappointment will be vented inappropriately, often deflected onto entirely innocent individuals who happen to cross our paths at the wrong time.

As part of our spiritual practice, we must learn to tolerate conflict. In the *Abhaya Sutta*, the Buddha clearly notes how important it is to address contentious issues with others, rather than navigating around conflict: "In the case of words that I know to be true and worthwhile, but not necessarily agreeable to others, I decide when the time is right to speak, and then I say them." So the Buddha was not one to mince words when they were necessary.

Of course expressing discontent can require courage. For some of us, because of temperament or history, we may feel threatened by any kind of tension and find conflict unbearable. In this case we may react without even thinking by blowing up, or alternately, fleeing or emotionally shutting down. In order to cultivate wise friendships, we are going to have to learn to work through those impulses. Thankfully there are strategies to employ during unavoidable conflict. These tools go back 2,500 years, and help us stay grounded and secure during tense encounters.

Clarity is our greatest asset during any contentious dialogue. We can use the breath, body, metta, or a visualization to keep ourselves calm, clear, and present during conflict. In chapter 15 we talked about remaining relaxed with our breathing. To stay calm doesn't mean that we lack resolve. When our bodies are relaxed and our breathing smooth, we become more supple. We are far more resilient this way than we are when armored and combative.

If we hope to feel, process, and work with emotions, we must meet them in the realm where we stand a chance of prevailing: feeling impulses in the body, rather than engaging with them as ideas. It is helpful for us to feel our feelings as physical sensations of hollowness or tension as we allow the states to play out. With practice, the body can safely hold any state of passion, from the very joyful to the very not. And by *hold*, I mean that we feel them in a way that allows us to observe the feelings without reacting to them.

We can also focus on feeling loving-kindness for the person to whom we are speaking, wishing all the while that they are happy and well. It may feel a bit disingenuous if we are not feeling heard, but extending goodwill to another person will actually help us to open up, to sympathize, empathize, and understand.

It may also be helpful to visualize something that you associate with calmness and equanimity. For my part I find it relaxing to remember and visualize various Buddhist renunciates I've met, especially those with personalities that radiate wisdom, compassion, and more than a little humor, such as Ajahns Sucitto, Amaro, Brahm, and Sundara.

Sometimes the best way to restore clarity during a conflict is to recognize an impasse, take a break, and get away to add some self-soothing to the safe-container process. This can mean going to a quiet place, such as a park, or doing something we find comforting. Sometimes we can't hold those feelings safely at work or home; we need to be somewhere or doing something that makes us feel more resourceful.

If none of these other things work, we can always rely on the voice of a supportive friend. It's our job as wise friends to emotionally regulate each other during such struggles.

Gradual, incremental revealing; knowing my boundaries, sticking to them, and not justifying them; developing skills to deal with conflict—these are the ways we enter into relationships without rewounding ourselves and, at the same time, learn how to develop a sense of confidence and courage to move forward in life.

Practice:
Communicating with a Partner

If after practicing the incremental approach to relationships, we experience an imbalance of negative interactions over positive, we can try to treat relational strife as follows.

Make a weekly time to meet with your partner and take turns sharing while being fully available to each other. This means that we do not interrupt our partner, and we don't spend their time talking preparing our response. In fact no verbal response need be given after the other has taken their turn. Quietly feeling what has been expressed, pausing, calmly waiting to speak is a strong practice that builds both intimacy and tolerance.

Each partner should speak to the following, in this order:

(1) News. We might believe our partners know what's occurring in our lives, but such things are not always apparent. They may not be aware of our experiences or plans, and so it's important to open each dialogue by reviewing what is going on with us.

(2) Aspirations. What restaurants would we like to try out? Where would we like to travel? Would we like to learn a new kind of yoga? Relationships thrive when both members can locate similar goals; in turn, we can provide mutual support as we explore these intentions.

(3) Requests. We are capable of change, and we can learn to adapt to others' wants and needs, and we are more likely to do this when these are clearly and kindly requested.

(4) Appreciation. People judge events and interactions on how they felt during the most intense moments, rather than reviewing the overall experience. Our last impressions of any exchange play

a major role in whether or not we'll be willing to return to an endeavor. So it's vital to end each time of intimacy by expressing recognition of each other's efforts and growth. If we are to stay together for the long haul, acknowledgment will play as deep a healing role as forgiveness, for it builds a sense that our endeavors are being observed and noted.

◄ **IV.**

Opting In for Liberation

18. SEEKING THE SUBLIME

ALL OF US HUMAN mammals face an ongoing dilemma. As we've discussed, the analytical, narrative, goal-oriented circuits of the left brain are disinclined to allow us to feel the internal, physiological emotions known by the right hemisphere; the left hemisphere produces thoughts, plans, fantasies, worries, anything to distract us from feeling sad or disappointed. This hemisphere has little concern for how our actions affect the world around us. Rather, it fixates on what we can accumulate or accomplish in life. It chases after what the Buddha referred to as "worldly winds that blow us about" but don't provide anything lasting: money, stature, job titles, reputations, short-term dopamine pleasures.

In the background of this awareness, our right hemisphere continues to send signals in the form of feelings. If I am lonely and isolated, I feel uncomfortable. If I do something to the detriment of the tribe I'm connected with, I feel sensations indicating guilt or shame: nausea, perhaps. If I do something that benefits others, the circuits of the right hemisphere use the chest and facial muscles to signal states of pride and buoyancy.

Twenty-first century capitalism has drifted further away from a right-hemispheric, holistic awareness toward a left-hemispheric fetishization of acquiring symbols such as wealth and fame. Furthermore, we've become increasingly dependent on a mechanistic view of the world: an understanding that the world contains assets that we can extract without any repercussions or penalty. We feel quite empowered to spray deadly pesticides on fields, then seem shocked when the population of bumblebees dies off or when our water table becomes polluted, because the left hemisphere thinks in terms of "self" and "others" and doesn't understand that all objects are interconnected in some way.

But as dire as the consequences of left hemispheric dominance have been to the ecosystem, it also takes its toll in our individual lives. Every single time we prioritize our career, our shopping habits, or our need for entertainment and distraction over connecting with others via the disclosure of authentic, vulnerable emotional states, it's almost as if we're saying, "It's only my left hemisphere, and the symbols of wealth and abundance it seeks, that matters. My right hemispheric needs—to feel securely connected with other people, to connect and hold the emotions I'm feeling—don't really matter."

Every time we distract ourselves from an emotion of loneliness, sadness, or frustration that arises, we're turning a deaf ear to a significant part of the brain that's saying, "Hey, I don't feel secure right now. I'm worried about this job change. I'm worried about this risk I'm taking." Each time we regard our procrastination as if it's a sign of laziness, instead of perceiving it to be the right hemisphere's way of pulling our attention away from something it finds scary and vulnerable, we're closing ourselves off to our emotional minds.

In essence, we are prone to turning a deaf ear to the significant messages our relational circuits are desperately sending us via the body, almost like flares shot up into the night sky by those lost at sea. As we become mired in the search for symbolic security, we're overlooking opportunities for real, deep contentment. Now, don't get me wrong; there's nothing wrong in accomplishing things, nor is it necessarily shallow to seek to fill life with a lot of experiences, so we can construct a satisfying life story. Few of us would consider the times that we went home at night to connect deeply with our loved ones as showing great purpose or narrative.

But while the right hemisphere's circuits don't seek to acquire external goals or create a great life story, what they do seek is just as important. As much as we may need financial security to survive, so must we establish emotional security. To be happy requires more than good genes; it requires work that benefits others and friends with whom we are empathetically connected.

For over a dozen years I've mentored a wide array of practitioners. They arrive presenting symptoms of depression, anxiety, agitation, all forms of suffering, yet they invariably request, at first, that the solution involve sitting alone on a cushion. They never want to have to vulnerably make new friends—for that is, of course, the most frightening thing for adults to do. We can be too easily thrilled with the left hemisphere's promise: "I can solve all our problems. Just let me read the right book; I'm sure it'll contain the perfect idea to understand why I'm unhappy, and that will solve the issue once and for all."

When we understand the difference between the left hemisphere's narrowly focused, conceptualizing cognition, and the right hemisphere's embodied, connected, contextual awareness, it becomes clear that we're underutilizing one half of our brains. We must rebalance.

The most efficient way to restore hemispheric balance is to connect with others in a manner in which we simply listen without judgment, where we empathize with rather than try to fix or solve each other's problems. When we say, "I feel jealous, envious, lonely, tired, bored, frustrated," and our friend replies with, "Yes, I feel that way, too. All the time," we expose an authentic state of being.

Another way to address neural imbalance is to develop a greater awareness of our bodies. The right hemisphere doesn't speak to us through ideas, through inner chatter. It speaks through those times our stomach gets tight, our shoulders clench with stress because we're taking on too much, and the emotional brain is saying, "Stop, downsize, let go of something; you're taking on too much."

Yet another way to develop hemispheric balance is to cultivate a state of transcendence, of awe and wonder—a state where you're experiencing something and not turning it into an idea or a story. The sublime. These are right hemispheric states; according to Dacher Keltner, psychology professor at UC Berkeley, wonder is a socializing emotion. It helps us work together, to appreciate the fact that we are all part of a single, interconnected environment, a planet that's amazing. In a state of transcendent awe we stop thinking of ourselves in terms of self and other, "me" and "adversaries"; we perceive ourselves as part of a much larger ecosystem.

In this state we transcend the left hemisphere's reductionist, abstract concepts. We no longer think in terms of isolated objects that are either to my advantage or disadvantage; rather, we appreciate an experience or encounter in its totality, for example a stunning vista—the Northern Lights, the Grand Canyon, a national park, waves crashing across a jagged coastline. Awe and wonder take in the entirety of a set of sensations, limited not just to the visuals and thoughts, but to the way our body feels, the external sensations of air, the aromas, sounds, tactile sensations. Everything that we experience in a moment is part of awe; it is the richness of sensory experience, after all, that allows us to transcend the limited, claustrophobic dimension of abstract, self-centered thought.

Transcendence slams the brakes on our fight, flight, or freeze sympathetic nervous system and reduces cytokines, which are linked to high blood pressure and compromised immune systems. It's very, very, very good for you to experience awe on a regular basis.

That feeling, I can't describe, just point to it, because awe, as a right hemispheric emotion, doesn't blend itself very well with language. But I remember when I was younger and travelling through Italy, and I was lost in Florence, and there's these . . . all the streets are sort of curved, and then there's this . . . You can't really see because the streets are very narrow, and you can't even really see the sky, and then you stumble out into this square, and there's this massive cathedral. And I was struck by the immensity of it and the smallness of myself, and the smallness of other people, and how awe inspiring it all was. Beyond words or ideas, such an experience just transcended all of the lesser thoughts of "I've got to get somewhere. I've got to find something." And it just suddenly burst through, yanking me out of the narrative of my life.

The sublime experience creates a breach in the stories that we're telling about where we were, where we're heading, what happened to us in the past, what's going to happen to us in the future; it blows all of that self-oriented thinking away. When we have that experience, we are in awe and we're actually deeply reconnecting with the right hemisphere of the brain. And we're really rewarding that part of the brain that doesn't see the world in terms of self and other, but sees just the world in terms of symbiotic connection. Sees the world in terms of something that we're not separate from, but something we're very much an iteration of, a part of, and deeply embedded in.

Unfortunately, we have a tendency to stumble upon something transformative, transcendent, larger than life and immediately, instead of being present, think in terms of narratives: future Facebook postings, stories we'll tell our friends back home. We transform the wholeness of the experience into an emblem that we can carry around and show others and turni the experience from a right-hemispheric event to a left-hemispheric reductionist story. What's next in the trip?

There are a few ways we can go about connecting with

awe: One, drop the devices and actually take some time at night to gaze at the sky or anything that's larger, that's spacious, that creates an entire feeling of context. Take a walk through nature. Easier said than done in New York City, of course.

Single out each day a routine that we do quickly and do it radically slowly, painfully slowly. On retreats, for instance, we have people walk, feeling the sensations of lifting up the foot, moving it forward, placing it down. When you take the "I need to get somewhere"—the goal, the left-hemispheric narrative—out of walking, you bring back awareness to the sensations of actually being alive, connecting with the ground.

Actually, even regular walking can create a sense of awe, a sense of wonder. Note the balance, all the minute adjustments that go into it. Visiting a museum, looking at great art, forces us to open to awe. Even if you don't like Jackson Pollock, when you stop in front of one of his paintings, there's absolutely no way to turn that experience into words because there's no figuration, there's no story, there's no idea being presented. It's just a recording of a man connecting directly with his canvas. Or the work of Agnes Martin, or of any other great artist who learned to express themselves not through obvious concepts.

I often seek a gateway to the sublime in focused, eyes-closed immersion in what I consider to be transcendent music. I remember the first time I heard Marvin Gaye's classic album *What's Going On*; the hairs on the back of my neck stood on end, my spine tingled, I felt both elated and slightly scared. The beauty of sounds ripped off the streets of the early '70s, Gaye's soulful voice and righteous lyrics, string sections and choruses soaring over R & B rhythms: it was a direct experiential route to the heart of this world. I had a similar experience seeing Steve Reich leading his excellent ensemble through his masterpiece "Music for 18 Musicians" and while dancing in wild abandon to the music of the Bad Brains or the Cro-Mags.

There are so many ways we can disconnect from our inner chatter and thought-generated fantasies, but I'll conclude with the most obvious: meditation. There's a 2,500-year old meditation of the Buddha in the *Cula-Sunnata Sutta* that I believe was specifically composed to cultivate states of transcendence, a wonder that lies far beyond the grasp of the narrowly focused conceptual mind, the profound.

Practice:
Meditation That Leads to the Transcendent State of Emptiness

If you'd like to practice this meditation, I'd like to suggest that you set aside at least forty minutes, preferably an hour. And please note that the meditation requires some use of visual imagination; don't worry about getting it right; just follow the instructions as best you can. Finally, know that the meditation is subtractive in nature; it's based on removing from awareness certain objects and focusing on the objects that remain. So as we move from one stage to the next, pay attention to which perceptions (sounds, etc.) remain available to the mind, and let go of the perceptions that have been cleared away.

Let's start with the first stage of awareness, which is based on our surrounding human landscape. For this stage, open your eyes and establish an open, unfocused awareness of the ordinary reality around you: the sights of the room you're sitting in (the walls and furniture, the floor); the sounds and aromas; feelings of contact made while sitting on the chair or cushion; the feeling of the body breathing. You can even extend your awareness beyond what's visible and allow into your awareness any memories you have of what's outside of the building you're presently situated in. Perhaps other buildings, a city or town.

Now let's venture on to the **second stage of the practice**: close your eyes, remove from memory the images of the room and buildings around you, and turn your attention to elements of the natural environment. Allow into the mind any images you have of the natural environment around you: land, forests of trees or desert tundras, lakes or oceans, wild animals such as deer or birds, mountains, open sky, whatever naturally arises. Whenever man-made objects appear in the mind—such as images of houses, buildings, cars and roads, gently release them. You're sustaining contemplation of the natural world.

Note how this second stage—reflections on nature—may feel more tranquil than the first stage—awareness of the human landscape. It's not as busy and demanding. This will be the process of the meditation: we'll simplify awareness in each ensuing stage, gently changing what's attended to by the mind.

For the third stage remove from your reflections awareness of living things—trees, plants, animals—and focus instead on the contact sensations you're making with the floor or chair beneath you. If you like, bring to mind the soil, ground, earth. This is our foundation, the material physical reality; you can even employ your imagination to be comprehensive: visualizing miles of continent or even the entire surface of the earth, a planet moving through a vast region of space.

This is where we move onto **the fourth stage**, what the Buddha called the formless realms—awareness essentially of the elements of our psyche that have no physicality. We enter this stage of the practice by removing our reflections of the ground and earth. So we drop the sensations of contact with the found, and allow the visual reflection of the earth floating in space to dissolve, leaving only a sense of the vast space that surrounds us.

At this point we want to establish in mind a sense of space without limits or boundaries. In the *Cula-*

Sunnata Sutta, the Buddha explains the practice as follows: "No longer attending to the perception of city, of nature, of the perception of earth, one attends to the undivided dimension of infinite space." We should spend some time in this domain, allowing our imagination to roam about in it, then broaden it to fill the boundless space. This part of the meditation is among the most challenging, as we're used to confining our sense of awareness to a limited field behind our eyes; it requires a great deal of practice and willingness to practice expanding our sense of "where I am" or "where the center of my consciousness resides." To feel consciousness as vast can feel a bit disconcerting, so this practice should be done slowly; feel free to return awareness to the sensations of the floor beneath you should you feel anxious or flustered.

To move on to **the fifth stage**, we withdraw attention from the sense of space, and turn awareness in on itself, focusing on the nature of consciousness itself. At this stage many practitioners struggle to understand the practice. Essentially this stage is achieved by turning attention to what recognizes space: consciousness. Of course, the mind will prefer to cling to what it's used to—if not objects, then at least a visual image of black space. Essentially the mind feels most comfortable visualizing something external to itself. Even though space is, of course, nothing, the mind will conceive of this nothing as outside itself, a place to inhabit. At this stage we're trying to let go of a sense of place or location and observe the sense of consciousness itself, filling with energy, dulling out, contained or vast.

The last stages of the meditation require no less courage: we withdraw attention from the nature of consciousness and open to a sense emptiness, a stage of awareness without ebb and flow, where things may happen but the mind pays no heed. In this stage we're nearing to what the Buddha said was the ultimate goal of the practice; instead of allowing the mind to contract around thoughts or images or fleeting sensations, we keep the mind open and spacious, containing everything but focusing on nothing.

At this point I'll let the Buddha describe what happens next:

> Your mind takes in pleasure and satisfaction; it settles into a themeless state of awareness. Note that anything that would disturb the mind, causing it to contract, is external to this awareness. Here we are in a state of emptiness that is transcendent and unsurpassed; there is nothing beyond this state of mind, and so you should train yourselves to achieve this state of release.

19. A MIND THAT CONTAINS EVERYTHING

ALL SPIRITUAL PRACTICE, especially meditation, fundamentally involves a change in outlook, in how we relate to the daily events of life. It's not about keeping something in mind, such as the breath, or pushing other things out of mind, such as worrying thoughts; it's essentially a purposeful alteration of how we respond to sensations, impressions, feelings, moods, and thoughts. The entire path of liberation depends upon supporting this transformation in attitude.

What point of view, or attitude, are we moving away from? The habit of identifying with our thoughts, feelings, and emotions. The default way we relate to being angry, disappointed, worried, depressed, anxious, or exhausted is to take these states personally, as predicaments that won't change naturally on their own unless we do something. We feel inclined to get involved, to either (1) control the world, including other people, in such as way as to make life as easy for us as possible, or (2) control our thoughts, feelings, and moods with the goal of creating an enduring, positive, pleasant state of mind. We want to feel good all the time, and we spend a lot of our energies trying to make everything feel pleasant.

But let's face it, despite all the self-help books and online spiritual courses and weekend retreats with gurus and yoga and healthy probiotic natural lifestyles, feeling swell all the time just isn't in the cards. We can save all the money we need, retire, get to the perfect beach with the perfect conditions, and bang, something goes wrong. An unpleasant memory arises, or a worry about our health, or loneliness, or clouds will arrive and bring with them torrential showers. It's not because we haven't stumbled across the right way to live, or the perfect getaway; it's simply that pleasant experiences cannot last.

Fortunately, if we don't take life's neutral and even, gulp, unpleasant moods and feelings personally, as states we must remove or repress, then we manage to attain something far greater than pleasant moods: we can develop some peace and calm. For while comfort isn't meant to last, there's a deep peace that arises from welcoming and exploring each state of mind, no matter how unpleasant. Liberation is when we turn the intention to "live and let live" inward, toward our own emotions, moods, thoughts.

To be emancipated is to develop a way to simply observe thoughts and emotions. The change in attitude we're seeking is quite the opposite of the working, busy mind, which is always putting out fires, dealing with crises, getting a handle on things, making a go of it, and so on. The need to fix and solve is okay at work, but if we bring it home and try to fix and solve our loved one's feelings, or our own feelings, we'll be stuck in an ongoing campaign that will never end.

Fortunately stress and suffering can be vastly lessened, scaled down to a place where life isn't something that has to be dealt with.

How do we achieve this? We observe and learn. What are the ways of greeting experience that create stress and agitation, and which are the approaches that reduce agitation? What are the attitudes and beliefs that produce peace, lack of agitating criticism and inner chatter, acceptance, and calmness? When are we not struggling with life? In short, we're not focusing on the content of mind—topics, concerns, fears, moods—but the way we greet and relate to these contents.

The only available orientation toward life that can cultivate calm abiding is *nonjudgmental, present-time awareness*. As we've discussed elsewhere, judgmental, or critical, awareness adds views and opinions—cognition—to our experience. And Killingsworth and Gilbert's study "A Wandering Mind Is an Unhappy Mind" demonstrates that we humans tend to spend almost as much time lost in thought as we stay focused on present-time tasks—yet being lost in thought creates distress.

So the question boils down to this: Can we stay with whatever we're experiencing? Can we experience life without commenting on it, adding to it, abandoning it? Can we stay with what's happening, without producing a virtual reality to replace our lived experience?

When we learn to really observe what's happening right now, we're invariably struck by how complete and full each moment is. There's nothing to push through or survive, for moments take care of themselves; they pass on their own. It's not necessary to develop patience, as that appears as a byproduct of observing what's happening rather than taking control.

Practice:
How Do We Practice When Life Really Sucks?

When we encounter the unpleasant or uncomfortable, we acknowledge it, then expand attention beyond that area, to sensations outside the discomfort. We always keep the mind as expansive as possible. For example, if a stressful thought about a conflict with a family member appears, we note the thought, then enlarge our awareness to include background sounds, or the sensations of the breath, or perhaps the lights flickering behind closed eyelids. If our stomach is knotted, we acknowledge sensations beyond the abdomen: perhaps comfortable feelings in our palms.

We can open our awareness. Rather than harboring a goal to get rid of anything—even fearful thoughts—we develop the capability to be with the thoughts, sounds, anxiety, alertness. We include everything that's present in an awareness that encompasses the entirety of this moment of experience. When we allow the mind to become truly open and flooded with present awareness, the sense of a self that persists from the past to the future wanes; all that remains is a sense of sensory completeness and freedom to fill space with consciousness. Any sense that awareness has a center begins to recede, along with the ideas of "me" and "not," and "mine" and "not mine."

When the mind is as vast as the sky, we make sense of experiences without relying on adding commentary but by receiving all feelings, emotions, sensations, memories, images. Possibilities open up; we are free to engage in different ways of conceiving ourselves, others, purpose. This is a way out of the habits and prisons of the mundane mind. In openness, space, time, self, and other are thrown into disarray. This is a practice of leaning into the completeness of each moment.

Eventually, as we put aside the need to do anything about experience, the observing mind becomes the core, underlying, foundational state of being. When we remove everything that comes and goes, we're left with awareness. Everything else—happy, sad, fear, anxiety, anger, envy, confusion—comes and goes. Awareness is constant, though unappreciated, as it's the body of water that contains all the ripples and waves that can stir us up. So the key isn't to focus on the ripples or waves, but on the lake itself, which always returns, eventually, to pristine and clear.

SELECTED BIBLIOGRAPHY

Books on Buddhism and the Dharma

Analayo. *Satipaṭṭhāna: The Direct Path to Realization*. Windhorse Publications, 2004.

Batchelor, Stephen. *Alone with Others: An Existential Approach to Buddhism*. New York: Grove Press, 1994.

Buddhadasa Bhikkhu. *Heartwood of the Bodhi Tree: The Buddha's Teaching on Voidness*. Boston: Wisdom Publications, 2014.

Buddhadasa Bhikkhu. *Me and Mine: Selected Essays of Bhikkhu Buddhadasa.*Sri Satguru Publications, 1991.

Brach, Tara. *Radical Acceptance: Embracing Your Life With the Heart of a Buddha*. New York: Bantam, 2004.

Chah, Ajahn. *Food for the Heart: The Collected Teachings of Ajahn Chah*. Boston: Wisdom Publications, 2002.

Hanson, Rick. *Buddha's Brain: The Practical Neuroscience of Happiness, Love, and Wisdom*. Oakland, CA: New Harbinger Publications, 2009.

Levine, Noah. *Against the Stream: A Buddhist Manual for Spiritual Revolutionaries*. New York: HarperOne, 2007.

Sucitto, Ajahn. *Meditation: A Way of Awakening*. Freely distributed pdf.

Thanissaro Bhikkhu. *The Wings to Awakening: An Anthology from the Pali Canon*. Free distribution, 1996.

Books on Psychology and Neuroscience

Bowlby, John. *A Secure Base: Parent-Child Attachment and Healthy Human Development*. New York: Basic Books, 1988.

Damasio, Anthony. *Descartes' Error: Emotion, Reason, and the Human Brain*. New York: Penguin Books, 2005.

Flores, Philip J. *Addiction as an Attachment Disorder*. Lanham, MD: Jason Aronson, Inc., 2011.

Fonagy, Peter, and Gyorgy Gergely, Elliot Jurist, and Mary Target. *Affect Regulation, Mentalization, and the Development of Self*. New York: Other Press, 2005.

Ledoux, Joseph. *The Emotional Brain: The Mysterious Underpinnings of Emotional Life*. New York: Simon & Schuster, 1998.

Lieberman, Matthew D. *Social: Why Our Brains Are Wired to Connect*. New York: Broadway Books, 2014.

McGilchrist, Iain. *The Master and His Emissary: The Divided Brain and the Making of the Western World*. New Haven, CT: Yale University Press, 2012.

Mitchell, Stephen A., and Margaret J. Black. *Freud and Beyond: A History of Modern Psychoanalytic Thought*. New York: Basic Books, 1996.

Phillips, Adam. *Winnicott*. Cambridge, MA: Harvard University Press, 1989.

Schore, Allan N. *Affect Regulation and the Repair of the Self*. New York: W.W. Norton & Company, 2003.

Wallin, David J. *Attachment in Psychotherapy*. New York: The Guilford Press, 2015.

Winnicott, D. W. *Playing and Reality*. New York: Routledge, 2005.

INDEX

A

Abhaya Sutta (Buddha), 209
acceptance, 92–93
accountability, 23–24
action
  emotions stimulating, 89–90
  taking, 19–20
  weighing death and, 38–39, 41
addictions
  avoiding feelings with, 105–6,
    117, 122
  Jake's story, 117–18
  repressed feelings stimulating,
    108–9
Adult Children of Alcoholics
  (Woititz), 159
AIM (Accept, Inquire, and
  Mother), 92–94
Anatta-lakkhana Sutta, 51, 184
anger
  alleviating, 104–5
  avoiding, 102–3
  facing, 106–8
  practice for, 111–12
  reacting with, 103–4
  types of, 101–2
annihilation anxiety, 82–83

anxiety
  effect of repressed, 87–90
  neurotic anxiety, 84–85
  practicing with, 186–88
  separation as source of, 83–84
  vulnerability and, 82–83
assadas, 32
atman, 49
attention, 67–68, 153–56
attitudes. *See brahmaviharas*
attunement, 161, 172–73
authenticity
  changes creating, 19–20
  living with, 7, 42–45
  pleasure not synonymous with,
    13–14
  verifying beliefs and values
    for, 18
avoidance coping, 86–87
awareness
  of attention, 67–68, 153–56
  breathing and bodily, 65–66
  constancy of, 233
  meditation for transcendent,
    224–28
  noting emotions in safe con-
    tainer, 128–30

practice of choiceless, 153–56
practicing inner, 90–91
Ayacana Sutta, 182–84

B

balance, 178–79, 184–85
body
　breathing and awareness of,
　　65–66
　integrating mind and, 59–64
　practice for relaxing, 176–77
　returning mind to emotional
　　body, 78–79
　strong feeling and sensations
　　of, 66–67
"bottom-up" process, 64
Brach, Tara, 125
brahmaviharas (sublime
　　attitudes)
　for anxious adults, 186–88
　applying, 185
　attachment styles, 189–90
　for avoidant in relationship,
　　188–89
　defined, 181
　equanimity practice, 190–91
　for secure adults, 185–86
brain
　interpreting external world,
　　58–59
　left-hemisphere characteristics,
　　121, 217, 218, 219–20
　mindfulness and effect on,
　　64–69
　processing emotions in,
　　120–21
　right-hemisphere characteris-
　　tics of, 67–68, 120–21, 217,
　　218–19, 220

ways of rebalancing, 220–21
breathing
　bodily awareness and, 65–66
　long exhalation practice,
　　176–77
　relieving aggressiveness with,
　　106
Buddha
　on addressing contentious
　　issues, 209
　compassionate teaching by,
　　183–84
　on friendships, 23
　Mara and shadow self of,
　　135–37
　response to *Anatta-lakkhana
　　Sutta,* 184
　on *yoniso manashikara,* 32
Buddhism
　books on, 235
　Western adaptation of, 4–5
busyness/workaholism, 98,
　　139–40

C

catastrophizing, 86
change
　accountability for, 23–24
　embracing, 34–35
　escaping daily routine for,
　　29–30
　fear of, 33–34
　lifelong practice of, 25
　making, 21–22
　noticed in personal bodies, 51
　role of mindfulness in, 64
　taking action, 19–20
　unconscious beliefs preventing,
　　31–33

choiceless awareness practice, 153–56
cleansing ritual practice, 177–78
codependency, 159–61
communicating
emotions, 105
with partner practice, 211–13
community
need for, 161, 164
supporting meditation with, 162–64
See also interpersonal connections
compartmentalization, 141–42
compassion (*karuna*)
defined, 182
goodwill and, 182–84
for self, 188
See also brahmaviharas
compulsive behaviors, 110–11
conflict
avoiding, 205–7
working with, 205–7
consumerism and fear of change, 27–29
craving (*tanha*), 82
creating connections, 172–75
cleansing ritual practice, 177–78
empathy, 175
keeping in touch, 172
labeling emotions practice, 177
long exhalation practice for, 176–77
maintaining balance, 178–79
seeing others and being seen by them, 172–73
self care, 176

sympathy, 173–74
understanding motivations, 165–66, 174
Cula-Sunnata Sutta, 224, 226–27
cultural influences, 53–54

D

Damasio, Antonio, 88
death
authentic living and, 42–45
awareness provided by, 40–41
grief of, 118–19
illusion of continuous identity, 51–56
inevitability of, 37–38
mindfulness of, 38–40, 45–46
defense mechanisms
avoidance coping, 86–87
burying feelings with, 97
busyness/workaholism, 98, 139–40
catastrophizing, 86
compartmentalization, 141–42
excessive sleep, 141
healing wounds protected by, 145–46
humor and minimizing, 99–100
idealizing, 142–44
intellectualization, 85
masking emotions, 98–99
projection, 98, 140
rationalizing, 144–45
denial
of death, 40
of inevitable, 168–69
depression, 74
desire, 14–15, 29
Dhammapada, 106

Dharma
  books on, 235
  five daily recollections, 45–46
discomfort, pushing away, 76–77
ditthi upadana, 85
dukkha vedana (disgust), 115

E
eating disorders, 142
embracing change, 34–35
emotions
  alleviating negative, 104–5
  anxiety, 82–85
  contagion of, 176
  disclosing your, 147–56
  facing, 106–8
  founded on feelings, 115–17
  identifying with, 229–30
  making sense of, 119–26
  masking, 98–99
  noticing underlying, 81–82
  observing thoughts and,
    230–31
  practice labeling, 177
  practices for, 126–30
  repressing, 132–33
  restoring clarity in, 209–11
  returning mind to emotional
    body, 78–79
  seeking friends' help with,
    163–64
  separating thinking and, 62–63
  spiritual bypass of, 106,
    113–17, 164
  unconscious beliefs, 31–33
  when to follow intuition and,
    88–90

See also feelings; personal emo-
    tional histories; *and specific
    emotions*
empathetic joy (*mudita*), 184
empathy
  defined, 175
  empathetic connection prac-
    tice, 164–66
emptiness, 71, 72–74
equanimity practice, 190–91
equanimity (*upekkha*), 178–79,
    184–85
excessive sleep, 141
experiences
  avoiding, 85–87
  figuring out one's, 59, 60, 61,
    62, 122–23
  making sense of painful,
    119–26
  meaning in, 52–53
  practice for painful, 232–33
  staying with one's, 229–32
  suppressing painful, 95–96,
    133–34

F
facing anger, 106–8
fear of change
  consumerism and, 27–29
  embracing change, 34–35
  facing fears, 33–34
  unconscious beliefs fueling,
    31–33
  feelings (*vedana*)
  allowing, 95–97
  anger, 100–104, 111–12
  burying, 97
  busyness/workaholism pre-
    venting, 98

compulsive behaviors, 110–11
cycle of inclinations, cravings,
   and, 81–82
emotions founded on, 115–17
of emptiness, 71, 72–74
humor and minimizing,
   99–100
important messages of, 117
information contained in, 89
masking emotions, 98–99
mindfulness of, 66–67
projection, 98, 140
repressing anxious, 83–84
signals of repressed, 108–9
See also shadow self
*Four Foundations of Mindfulness
   Sutta,* 66
Frankl, Viktor, 13
friendships
avoiding with meditation,
   163–64
communicating with partner,
   211–13
discerning wise friends,
   198–99
finding support in wise, 106–8
importance of, 193–94
incremental revealing in,
   199–203
need for, 7–8, 159–60, 164
relying on friends, 23
setting secure boundaries,
   203–4
viewing as commodity, 194–96
working with conflict in,
   205–7
full disclosure
author's emotional inventory,
   148–52

practice of choiceless awareness, 153–56
process during, 151–52
sharing shadows with others,
   147–48

G

Gaddula Sutta, 50
Gaye, Marvin, 223
Gazzaniga, Michael, 51–52, 68
Geoff, Ajahn, 178
Gilbert, Daniel, 62, 231
goodwill
compassion and, 182–84
empathetic joy when practicing,
   184
importance of cultivating, 181
Gotami, Kisa, 169–70
grief, 101–2, 118–19
guidance, 69–70
gut feelings, 66–67, 89

H

habitual behaviors
anxiety and, 82–84
constructing false self, 131–33
defense mechanisms as, 85–87
noticing, 81–82
practice for compulsive,
   110–11
practicing inner awareness,
   90–91
repressing, 87–90
healing, 125–26, 145–46
hindrances. *See* defense
   mechanisms
humor, 99–100

I

idealizing, 142–44
identity
  cultural influences on, 53–54
  illusion of continuous, 51–56
  language and concept of,
    47–48
  letting go of, 55–56
  meaning and purpose via,
    49–51
  personal narrative about,
    96–97
  self-hood and, 50–51
illusion of continuous identity,
  51–56
impermanence, 170–71
inclinations (*namarupa*), 81–82
inner awareness. *See* awareness
inquire, 93
insomnia, 122
intellectualization, 85
interpersonal connections
  brahmaviharas for, 185–89
  communicating with partner,
    211–13
  discerning wise friends,
    198–99
  empathetic connection practice,
    164–66
  healing and, 125–26
  importance of, 159–62
  incremental revealing in,
    199–203
  as support for meditation, 163
  survival and, 131
  ways to create, 172–75
  working with conflict in,
    205–7
  See also creating connections

Interpreter, 51, 53, 54, 68
intuition, 88, 115–16

J

James, William, 124
"just this" practice, 76, 77

K

Kalama Sutta, 16
Kapleau, Philip, 3
karuna. See compassion
keeping in touch, 172
Killingsworth, Matthew, 62, 231
kindness toward self, 24–25
"King Sakka's Demon," 107
Korda, Josh
  disclosing shadow self, 148–52
  life story of, 1–7
  on living authentic life, 7–9

L

labeling emotions practice, 177
language, 47–48
letting go of identity, 55–56
Levine, Noah, 6–7, 22
livelihood, 21
living with purpose
  accountability for change,
    23–24
  acquiring objects, 14–15, 29
  creating meaning, 15–17
  death and, 37–38, 40–41
  finding life's purpose, 17–18
  kindness toward self, 24–25
  lifelong practice of, 25
  making changes for, 21–22
  relying on wise friends, 23
  risking illusions when, 15–16
  self motivation tips, 24–25

weighing actions, 38–39, 41
work benefiting others, 21
long exhalation practice,
    176–77

M

Man's Search for Meaning
    (Frankl), 13
Mara, 92, 135–37
meaning
    emotional processing of, 62–63
    expectation of finding, 47–48
    finding one's, 15–16, 49–51
    integrating, 124–25
    multiple levels of, 123
    perceptions of experience and,
        52–53
    taking setbacks personally,
        169–70
meditation
    changing outlook in, 229–32
    leading to transcendent state,
        224–28
    mindfulness of death in, 45–46
    overemphasis on, 162–63
    supporting with community,
        162–64
    See also practice
mentalizing, 165–66, 174
metta, 182
Milarepa, 138
mind
    integrating body and, 59–64
    returning to emotional body,
        78–79
    See also thinking
mindfulness
    of attention, 67–68

breathing and bodily awareness,
    65–66
of death, 38–40
of feelings and sensations,
    66–67
finding guidance with, 69–70
integrating mind and body,
    59–64
of interpretations of external
    world, 68–69
Western practice of, 3–5
minimizing feelings, 99–100
mother in AIM practice, 93–94
mudita (empathetic joy), 184
"Music for 18 Musicians," 224

N

namarupa (inclinations), 81–82
negativity bias, 170–72
neurotic anxiety, 84–85
Nibbedhika Sutta, 116
noting emotions in safe con-
    tainer, 128–30

P

Padhana Sutta, 136–37
painful experiences
    making sense of, 119–26
    practice for, 232–33
    suppressing, 95–96, 133–34
patience, 20, 25
people
    creating boundaries with, 108,
        203–4
    keeping in touch with, 172
    seeing and being seen by,
        172–73
    sympathy with, 173–74, 175

understanding motivations, 165–66, 174

worrying about opinions of other, 171–72

personal emotional histories

anxiety in, 82–84

defense mechanisms in, 85–87

noticing details of, 81–82

practicing inner awareness, 90–91

results of anxiety-based repression, 87–90

pleasant feeling (*sukkha vedana*), 115

practice

AIM, 92–94

choiceless awareness, 153–56

cleansing ritual, 177–78

communicating with partner, 211–13

embracing change, 34–35

emotions, 126–30

empathetic connection, 164–66

equanimity, 190–91

facing fears, 33–34

labeling emotions practice, 177

lifelong, 25

long exhalation practice, 176–77

meditation leading to transcendent state, 224–28

mindfulness of death, 45–46

RAIN, 126–28

returning to emotional body, 78–79

understanding compulsive behaviors, 110–11

Welcome Mara!, 137–38

when life really sucks, 232–33

projection, 98, 140

psychology and neuroscience bibliography, 236

R

RAIN practice, 126–28

rationalizing, 144–45

rebalancing brain, 220–21

Reich, Steve, 224

relationships

accountability in, 23–24

attachment styles of, 189–90

commodification of, 194–96

communicating with partner practice, 211–13

conflict in, 205–11

discerning wise friends, 198–99

empathizing with others, 185–86

equanimity practice for, 190–91

finding support in wise, 106–8

incremental revealing in, 199–203

need for secure, 7–8

practice for anxious adults, 186–88

practice for secure adults, 185–86

practice for those avoidant in, 188–89

relying on friends, 23

See also interpersonal connections

repression

anxiety based on, 87–90

effect of emotional, 95–96,
133–34
learning to repress emotions,
132–33
signal anxiety and, 108–9
risk taking in friendships,
199–203

S

Sambodhi Sutta, 193
Sangha. *See* community
sanna, 61
sanna-Vipallasa, 61
sati (inner awareness), 91
security, 186–88
self care, 176
self motivation tips, 24–25
self-acceptance, 8, 92–93
self-hood and identity, 50–51
separation anxiety, 82–83
shadow self
author's disclosure of, 148–52
creation of, 133–34
defense mechanisms against,
139–46
handling one's, 134–37
practice for, 137–38
sharing with others, 147–48
signals of repressed feelings,
108–9
spiritual bypass of, 106,
113–17, 164
sleep
excessive, 141
insomnia, 122
somatic markers, 66–67
spiritual bypass, 106, 113–17,
164

sublime attitudes. *See brahma-viharas*
suffering
denying inevitable, 168–69
failing to recognize impermanence, 170–71
kinds of, 167–68
taking setbacks personally,
169–70
ways we cause, 168–72
worrying about people's opinions, 171–72
sukkha vedana (pleasant feeling),
115
Sumedho, Ajahn, 76
support for changes, 20
suppression. *See* repression
Suzuki, Shunryu, 3
sympathy, 173–74

T

thinking
emotions and sensations prior
to, 124
enforcing identity with language and, 47–48
figuring out experience by, 59,
60, 61, 62, 122–23
finding transcendent meaning
in, 74–75, 77
gaps between thoughts, 76
identifying with, 229–30
influence on perceptions,
52–53
integrating emotions with,
59–64
making sense of emotions,
119–26

observing emotions and,
230–31
practicing inner awareness, 91
returning to emotional body,
78–79
separating from emotions,
62–63
thoughts. *See* thinking
Three Pillars of Zen, The (Kapleau), 3
transcendence
creating transformative
moments, 221–24
finding transcendent meaning,
74–75, 77
of meaninglessness, 15–16
meditation leading to, 224–28
rebalancing brain via, 220–21
transformative moments,
221–24
translations, xvii-xviii

U
unconscious emotional beliefs,
31–33
Upadda Sutta, 193
upekkha (equanimity), 178–79,
184–85

V
vedana. See feelings

Vedana Sutta, 116
viraga (tranquil dispassion), 116
vulnerability, 8, 82–83

W
*Wandering Mind Is an Unhappy
Mind, A* (Killingsworth and
Gilbert), 62, 231
Watts, Alan, 3
Way of Zen, The (Watts), 3
Welcome Mara! practice, 137–38
Welwood, John, 106
What's Going On, 223
wise friends, 201–3
Woititz, Janet, 159
wonder, 220–22
work
benefiting others, 21
busyness/workaholism, 98,
139–40
World Happiness Report, 28
worrying, 171–72

Y
yoniso manashikara (deep understanding), 32

Z
Zen Mind, Beginner's Mind
(Suzuki), 3

ABOUT THE AUTHOR

 Since 2005 **JOSH KORDA** been the guiding teacher of Dharma Punx NYC and is a fully empowered Dharma teacher in the Against the Stream lineage. In addition to his weekly classes, and meditation retreats for both institutions, he has led online and residential retreats for *Tricycle* and *Lion's Roar* magazines. Josh is widely known for his podcast, which has over 1.4 million downloads, and has written numerous articles on insight meditation for *Tricycle*, *Lion's Roar*, *Buddhadharma,* and *Huffington Post.* Josh can also be seen on Viceland TV Channel's public-service announcements, and his Dharma talks are broadcast weekly on WBAI radio.

WHAT TO READ NEXT
FROM WISDOM PUBLICATIONS

Hardcore Zen
Punk Rock, Monster Movies, and the Truth About Reality
Brad Warner

"*Hardcore Zen* is to Buddhism what the Ramones were to rock and roll: A clear-cut, no-bulls**t offering of truth."
—Miguel Chen, Teenage Bottlerocket

One City
A Declaration of Interdependence
Ethan Nichtern

"Resonant and refreshing."—*The American Prospect*

A New Buddhist Path
Enlightenment, Evolution, and Ethics in the Modern World
David R. Loy

"This gripping, important, and ultimately heartening book by David Loy is a wake-up call for Buddhists and everyone else on how to respond to the current multiple crises."
—Lila Kate Wheeler, author of *When Mountains Walked*

Awakening from the Daydream
Reimagining the Buddha's Wheel of Life
David Nichtern
Foreword by Lodro Rinzler

"A wonderful extension of the powerful Dharma teachings of Chögyam Trungpa Rinpoche. The transmission of these ancient lineages is intact in David's hands as he continues to update the traditional Buddhist teachings and make them ever more accessible to the contemporary audience."
—Ram Dass, author of *Be Here Now*

What's Wrong with Mindfulness (And What Isn't)
Zen Perspectives
Edited by Robert Rosenbaum and Barry Magid

"This book is the best thing I've read on mindfulness and the mindfulness movement."—David Loy, author of *A New Buddhist Path*

Zen Under the Gun
Four Zen Masters from Turbulent Times
J. C. Cleary

"These four generations of Chinese masters indeed taught amid social turbulence. These luminous teachings, translated clearly for the first time, remain informative for our own troubled period."—Taigen Dan Leighton, translator of *Dogen's Extensive Record*

Buddha at the Apocalypse
Awakening from a Culture of Destruction
Kurt Spellmeyer
Foreword by Robert Thurman

"*Buddha at the Apocalypse* is easy-going, well written, and solidly reasoned—and lively in the way it interweaves Biblical analysis, Zen literature, and Western philosophy and sociology with popular culture and deep wisdom. I am delighted to greet this important and meaningful work."—from the foreword by Robert A. F. Thurman

About Wisdom Publications

Wisdom Publications is the leading publisher of classic and contemporary Buddhist books and practical works on mindfulness. To learn more about us or to explore our other books, please visit our website at wisdompubs.org or contact us at the address below.

Wisdom Publications
199 Elm Street
Somerville, MA 02144 USA

We are a 501(c)(3) organization, and donations in support of our mission are tax deductible.

Wisdom Publications is affiliated with the Foundation for the Preservation of the Mahayana Tradition (FPMT).